THE SINGING THING too

D1600535

Also by John L. Bell, available from GIA Publications, Inc.:

THE SINGING THING
A case for congregational song (G-5510)

The first of two books addressing the "whys" and "hows" of congregational
singing. Unapologetically anecdotal, it deals not with musical theories but
with the reasons why people sing and how best to enable them to do so.

This highly accessible analysis by John L. Bell, one of the world's leading
experts on congregational song, offers ten persuasive answers to the question
"Why do we sing?" Each is explored with a wealth of illustration and
practical insight born of 20 years' experience in this field.

A ROAD TO ROAM
A way of celebrating sacred space (G-6959)

SWEET HONEY & HARD PLACES
Prayer services based on the Psalms (G-6788)

THE LOVE WHICH HEALS
A service of grieving and gratitude for those who have been recently bereft
(G-6138)

PICTURES OF GOD
An act of worship about images (G-6330)

REMEMBER ME TODAY
A Good Friday reflection (G-6165)

A WEE WORSHIP BOOK (G-4425)

JESUS AND PETER
Off-the-record conversations (G-5288)

CLOTH FOR THE CRADLE
Worship resources and readings for Advent, Christmas and Epiphany
(G-5109)

STAGES ON THE WAY
Worship resources for Lent, Holy Week and Easter (G-5110)

PRESENT ON EARTH
Worship resources on the life of Jesus (G-6021)

G-6918

THE SINGING THING too
Enabling congregations to sing

John L. Bell

GIA PUBLICATIONS, INC.
CHICAGO

Copyright © 2007 John L. Bell/Wild Goose Resource Group
First published in North America by
GIA Publications, Inc.,
7404 S. Mason Ave., Chicago, IL 60638, USA.
www.giamusic.com
Exclusive North American distributor

ISBN 978-1-57999-690-1
Cover design © 2007 Graham Maule/Wild Goose Resource Group

All rights reserved. No part of this publication may be reproduced in any form or
by any means, including photocopying or any information storage or retrieval
system, without written permission from the publisher.

Permission to reproduce any part of this work in North America should be sought from
GIA Publications, Inc.

Printed by GIA Publications, Inc.

CONTENTS

Fondly dedicated to
the late Marion Fulton Lamberton,
my mother,
who sang to me that I might sing with others.

Introduction

When the late Sir Thomas Beecham and Leonard Bernstein asked me to write this volume, I declined because I wasn't old enough. Actually, they never asked me, but I thought the sight of their names might encourage some people to read the Introduction, a thing I seldom do myself.

Writing this book was not easy.

In *The Singing Thing 1*, I promised a subsequent volume which would deal with the 'how to' issues as regards congregational song. But trying to describe techniques in words is much more difficult than demonstrating them in action. That will become evident in chapter 2 where I found myself trying to find language to describe practices such as signing (rather than singing) tunes which are second nature to my colleagues and me, but defy verbalisation.

In addition, the fact that this book will be published on both sides of the Atlantic and read by people of different denominations creates the kind of linguistic difficulty which Winston Churchill famously pointed to when he spoke of the UK and the USA being separated by a common language.

For the innocent, it might be sufficient to state that in North America minims and crotchets could be the names of tropical gold-fish as far as music readers are concerned. Half-notes and quarter-notes are the order of the day. Similarly, some tunes change names when they go across the Atlantic: *Amazing Grace* becomes *New Britain*, and words such as 'congregation' – which most UK church-goers associate with those who sit in pews – may be taken by American Roman Catholics to refer to a sisterhood of nuns. Where an American congregation understands 'the Assembly' as those who gather for worship, Scottish Presbyterians use that term solely to refer to an annual gathering in Edinburgh for ecclesiastical governance.

So, dear reader, be prepared to have your musical, denominational and aesthetic sensitivities tramped on as you wend your way through these pages. But also be prepared to try things out. For this is a starter pack rather than a blueprint.

Everyone I know who teaches songs to congregations (or assemblies) uses a different approach. Teaching a song, like preaching a sermon, is an exercise in communicating truth through personality and these pages will be useless unless your interest in getting people to sing weds your unique personality to the suggestions that follow.

Nothing here is abstract theory. Everything that is written has been put into practice, and my gratitude to the groups of worshippers I have led and to my colleagues who have travelled the road with me will run deep for ever. My deep gratitude is also expressed to Sandra Kramer of Wild Goose Publications for her care in preparing the manuscript, and to several other colleagues whose comments have ensured that – as with all WGRG material – this is more than the work of one mind.

John L. Bell, 20th April 2006

Lion-taming for lambs or sheep-rearing for tigers

... something to do with the difference between a choir and a congregation

Seasoned authors say that the first line of a novel is sometimes the most important. Not being a novelist, I thought I'd go for a first chapter title.

This book has nothing to do with animal husbandry whatsoever but, for some people, the thought of teaching a congregation is more daunting than either of the above. Some musicians are threatened by the size of a congregation and, despite years of professional training, feel personally inadequate when asked to enable a large assembly to sing. Others, fed up with the discourteous noises issuing from a choir of three aged and infirm altos, can't wait to get their hands on a larger group and expose a degree of extroversion which is beyond the ability of Myers-Briggs or the Enneagram to interpret.

The fact is that most church musicians spend most of their time dealing with choirs. That – as regards vocal repertoire – is what many who have been trained in liturgical music will have spent years studying.

They may require choristers to sit in uncomfortable hard-backed seats which discourage slouching. They may require their singers to stand for much of the rehearsal, to scribble down tempo and breathing marks in pencil in the margins, to indulge in the sacred art of vocal kinesiology, otherwise known as warm-up exercises. They may even encourage their charges to contort their faces as if modelling for horror masks.

And all of this is worthy and – for some choirs – more of this is needed. But not for congregations.

The simple reason is that, to put it crudely, a choir and a congregation are different beasts. To treat the second as if it were the first is to be both insulting and unprofessional. In the same way, we would not expect an expert in ornithology speaking to an audience of twitchers (bird watchers) to use the same approach as when lecturing a class of post-graduate zoology students on the digestive tract of the bald eagle. To change the simile into another animal metaphor, it's horses for courses.

So I begin not with how to teach an assembly, but with a re-sensitising expedition into the difference between a choir and a congregation. First are some observations gleaned from fifteen years' experience of asking professional musicians and laypeople the question:

What differentiates a choir from a congregation?

1. The choir believes it can sing and the congregation knows it can't

The cynic will immediately take this to mean that the congregation knows that the choir can't sing. That may be true in some places, but what is more common is the fact that choirs have a self-confidence in music-making which far outstrips that of the congregation. (The exceptions, of course, are Sub-Saharan Africans, Mennonites and a fair number of Methodists.)

If the choir sings well, it will be congratulated. In some churches it may even be greeted with applause. But who encourages the song of the people? Indeed, which of you reading this have ever been in a church where the musician or the worship leader has unpatronisingly shown appreciation for the congregation's song?

In *The Singing Thing Part 1*, we noted how one in four people in many Western countries don't sing because they believe they can't. And that belief is inevitably grounded in a comment made to them when they were young. The same happens with a congregation.

Ten years ago one of my Wild Goose Resource Group colleagues and I worked for a while in a local parish where the rumour the congregation believed about itself was that it couldn't sing. And every Sunday people stood up to prove the truth of the rumour. There was little or no sound apart from the electronic organ. It transpired, on investigation, that there was nothing wrong with the people's voices. But a number of years previously they had had a 'musical' minister who on more than one occasion stated from the pulpit that the congregation couldn't sing. They believed his presumed authoritative verdict, and the self-confidence of the people's song evaporated.

Congregations, like choirs, need affirmation not discouragement.

2. The choir performs, the congregation listens

This theatrical understanding of music is sometimes encouraged by the sheer physical design of the church.

There may be a raised chancel area on which the principal players act out their roles. There may be an elevated podium dramatically perched above the congregation's heads from which preaching takes place. There may be ornate decoration or distinctive drapes and a special place set apart for instrumental and vocal musicians.

In contrast, for the congregation there will be rows of seats, varying in comfort and outlook but all facing the front. No wonder we sometimes look on worship as if it were a staged performance with the majority of those present being the audience.

But such an understanding leaves no room for God.

If we are going to validate the metaphor of worship as theatre, we have to think of everyone being on stage, from the acne-encrusted adolescent who breathes boredom and is reticent to sing, to the rich businessman who believes that his substantial covenant exempts him from everything communal. All of us – not just the choir and ministerial team – all of us are on the stage and God is in the audience. And everything is done primarily for the attention and enjoyment of the Almighty, not the sermon-tasters or amateur music critics in the back pews.

This, I suggest, is the mentality behind the music of Bach whose church cantatas were not sophisticated works of genius for the musically gifted to perform while the musically illiterate were meant to sit spellbound. He, who ended his manuscripts with the letters *AMGD* (*Ad Maiorem Gloriam Dei* – to the greater Glory of God) developed his cantatas around hymn tunes known to the congregation, and sometimes he would have the chorale sung by choir and congregation together, all voices uniting in praise of their Maker.

In worship God expects every voice to play its part.

3. The choir's music is perceived to be more important than the congregation's

In truth it is not more important, just different.

Granted, there are some traditions, notably the Orthodox and High Anglican, where certain services will be dominated by choral singing, but that is the outworking of a theology which sees the choir doing for God on behalf of the congregation what the congregation cannot do. It is not a matter of musical superiority, but of complementarity.

In the Psalms we find introductory ascriptions indicating that this or that poem is 'for the chief musician' or 'for the choir'. But such words, which post-date the original poems, are more speculative than authoritative. If we look at the text of the psalms we will see that for God the primary instrument in worship is the voice of the people.

It is not all choirs, or all praise bands, or all pipe organs, that are repeatedly called on to 'Praise your Maker!' and 'Sing to the Lord a new song!' but 'All people' as in Psalm 100, or 'All heavenly powers, servants of God, creatures of earth, places and you, my soul' as in Psalm 102.

The only time Jesus praises a musical contribution is in the temple precincts, days before the Passover. But it is not the practised voices of the temple choir he extols. No, it is the raw and rasping voices of children singing with gusto what their parents had sung the day before as they welcomed pilgrims arriving for the festival: 'Hosanna to the Son of David!' (Matt 21:15)

St Paul, on the few occasions when he alludes to music, regards it both as an individual activity – 'I will sing with the Spirit' (1 Cor 14:15) – and as a communal activity of the whole church – 'Sing psalms, hymns and spiritual songs' (Ephesians 5:19).

And just to round off this mini biblical tour de force, let us not forget the picture of heavenly music-making which the writer of the Revelation (Apocalypse) offers. Here is really egalitarian praise:

I heard every creature in heaven, on earth,
in the world below and in the sea –
all living beings in the universe –
and they were singing:
   'To him who sits on the throne
   and to the Lamb

be praise and honour, glory and might
for ever and ever.' (Revelation 5:13)

Does this undermine revered traditions of choral singing? No, it puts them in context. They represent a specialised contribution within the overall offering of the people's praise.

The presumed superiority rather than complementarity of the choir has not always gone unchecked. In post-Reformation Europe, specialised music for a gifted few was sometimes discouraged, savagely in Scotland where up to 80% of pre-Reformation choral manuscripts were destroyed. In such circumstances music came under the leadership (or tyranny) of a precentor, a man who chose the tunes and led the singing of metrical psalms. Sometimes, for the benefit of the illiterate (who were thicker on the ground in England than in Scotland due to the suppression of the monastic seats of learning by Henry VIII) the precentor sang the words a line at a time on a monotone before the congregation responded with the same dismembered text to a fragment of his chosen tune.

Later, in the 19th century when choirs began to be established in some Calvinist denominations, guidelines were drawn up regarding their purpose and behaviour. Here are four regulations from the document permitting a choir in Free St Andrew's Church, Kilmarnock:

a) The Choir may practise other suitable music, but their chief attention shall be to psalmody.

b) The Choir will not meet separately when the precentor is holding the *congregational* practice.

c) No one may join the choir unless permitted first to do so by the Psalmody Committee.

d) While the choir may consist of any number, only about twelve shall act at one time as such in the regular church service.

The reason for the fourth regulation was that the governing elders feared the new musical association might become apart from the congregation rather than be a part of it ... a not altogether unjustified apprehension.

Just for a moment, let us think of the act of worship less as theatre and more as an orchestral concert. If the main work is Tchaikovsky's *Piano Concerto No. 1*, a dexterous soloist will be required. But he or she will be of no effect if there are not cellos and double basses, bassoons and tubas, sometimes indistinguishable, but essential to the overall sound, especially in those bars where the piano is silent.

So, in worship, the musical offering of specialists is an integral but not independent feature of the liturgy.

4. A choir rehearses

Now we are moving from the philosophical to the practical.

No self-respecting director of music would decide half way through a Sunday morning eucharist that an appropriate communion anthem might be 'And the Glory of the Lord' from Handel's *Messiah* and then proceed to circulate the music to the unsuspecting choristers. If mutiny did not ensue, selective cardiac arrest might.

Yet we presume that it is by the alchemy of osmosis that a congregation should be able to sing immediately a song they have never rehearsed! And worse, if they prove their ineptitude the musical sophisticats respond by miaowing their disapproval.

Later we will look in detail at how a congregation can be rehearsed, but let it be sufficient for the moment to note that if music is offered for and to the glory of God, all who offer it should be enabled to give of their best.

5. A choir reads music, many pew occupants don't

Absolutely true, though the North American practice of having pew hymnals in four-part harmony sometimes suggests the contrary.

This, however, is not to suggest that those who do not read staff notation are musically unsophisticated. Where would the great traditions of Celtic folk-music, black Gospel singing, jazz or even Country & Western be if every performer had to be a music reader? And how full would opera-houses be if the prevailing wisdom was that only those who could read the full score of *The Magic Flute* were worthy to attend?

The truth is that many non-notation readers are very musically astute and have a capacity to learn and remember which leaves some of us musically literate creatures in the shade.

I think, for example, of a woman called Edna who had spent the first thirty-five years of her life in a hospital for the mentally handicapped simply because that was the establishment in which she had been born. Over three decades later she was released into the community and soon exhibited social inadequacy.

She and others who attended the same Adult Training Centre in Glasgow came to a Music, Art and Drama week on Iona, where most of the participants were fully functional and 'gifted' young adults. Edna brought the only musical instrument she possessed – a harmonica.

Before long, everyone was in awe of her as she showed her dexterity in playing exactly whatever she heard and revealed her hitherto unrecognised gift of perfect pitch. Equally, her musically illiterate colleagues from the Adult Training Centre amazed the choir director when they came along to a rehearsal of a choral work by Malcolm Williamson and learned the harmony lines by rote with greater accuracy than the musically literate did by sight reading.

How can this be? The simple fact is that music readers learn primarily by their eyes, and non-readers primarily by their ears.

If I am rehearsing a choir and I discover an alto is singing an F♯ when it should be an F♮, I may alert the whole section to the mistake by saying,

'Altos, in the fourth stave (system), bar two at the third beat, your note is an F♮, not an F♯. Could you fix that next time?'

If next time I hear the same mistake, I might become a little more forceful:

'Altos, one of you is receiving a message from her eyes which is not being transmitted by the brain to the vocal cords. In bar two of the second stave it's an F♮, not an F♯.'

And if it happens again ...

'Mrs Johnstone, in Christian love, would you please sing the proper note!'

For unless I draw Mrs Johnstone's attention to her error, she will continue to make it. She is reading a sharp as a natural and it is not her voice that is the culprit but her eyes.

Non-music-readers use their ears. I know this because when teaching without music, I frequently ask people how they have been able to learn a long tune and sing it accurately. Inevitably, someone will reply, 'I remembered what you demonstrated and I listened to the people around me.'

If we but think of it, the oldest songs and hymns in our repertoire will have been learned in this way. No mother or grandmother required the child on her lap to understand crotchets and quavers, bar lines and tempo markings before learning *Twinkle, Twinkle, Little Star*. And, marvel of marvels, fifty years later, we will still be able to sing these early songs, although we may well have forgotten the tune to the new hymn we sang from printed music last Sunday morning.

Years ago, I transcribed songs from a South African friend of mine, George Mxadana. Like many of his fellow countrymen, he was able to sing soprano, alto, tenor and bass parts with equal ease. I knew he conducted a choir, the Imolanji Kantu Choral Society of Soweto, and asked whether they were all music readers. He said he had no idea; they all learned by rote – everything from South African freedom songs to Handel's *Israel in Egypt*. I doubted his claim.

Then, in 2004 I attended a concert celebrating the 10th anniversary of democracy in South Africa. It was held in the Barbican Hall, London and it featured the Imolanji Kantu Choral Society who sang a lesser known (and rather unexciting) choral work by Mendelssohn word perfect without a music score in anyone's hands. They then performed a much more complex piece by a contemporary South African composer with equal ease.

Why is it, I wondered, that so many British choirs would baulk at the prospect of singing an eight-bar Taizé chant without the music, when these Africans can manage an oratorio?

Perhaps some of the most 'musically gifted' among us are those who would never think of describing themselves as such.

6. A choir sits together, a congregation sits apart

... and this explains why so many congregations are reticent to sing.

Here's a simple, but relatively unknown, rule of thumb: if you sit more than three feet (91.44 centimetres) away from someone you'll not sing in case they hear you. If you sit closer than three feet you will sing because you hear them. (Moral: always take a measuring tape to church.)

The way we sit either enables or disables congregational song, and though some stalwarts might want to sit where their grandmothers once did, even though it means there are demi-acres of empty seats all around them, this kind of privatisation of space has to be discouraged. Apart from anything else, the Church at worship is the Body of Christ and it should neither look dismembered nor suggest to the outsider that each worshipper suspects that all the others have a communicable disease.

Numerous churches have discovered that when the heating

breaks down and a smaller hall has to be used, or when the congregation is decamped for renovation work, the strange and more intimate temporary worship space often produces a greater sense of community and a more fulsome kind of singing than the usual place of worship.

For fifteen years I rented the former caretaker's house of a large Victorian church which had 1400 seats and a congregation of around 60 who sat like the scattered tribes of Israel. A new pastor encouraged people to sit together and occupy the front six pews.

The musical advantage was palpable. I can attest to it because from the bathroom in my house, under the previous configuration, you could only hear the organ playing. But when people were brought close together, their sound became clearly voluble, in addition to which sitting together vastly improved the learning of new congregational songs.

7. The choir has a music leader, the congregation hasn't

But there is no reason why this should remain so.

Admittedly, in churches where responsorial psalms are sung, there are people called cantors who introduce the short sung response to the psalm, sing the verses and then summon the congregation to sing the response.

But a congregational or pastoral musician has to do more. She or he has the great privilege and possibility of standing before a congregation, implicitly indicating that the voice of the people is a singular instrument which deserves to be utilised in worship to its best ability. He or she will enter into a relationship with the congregation whereby it is not the organist's bald head sticking above the console or the lead guitarist's selection of garish rings which symbolises musical leadership, but the voice of somebody who is encourager and enabler: the voice not of a precisionist but of an enthusiast; the voice not of professional prickliness but of nurturing friendship.

Sunday morning showers and weight loss through music

... something to do with teaching technique

The 29th Sunday in Ordinary.
The Church of St Polly and St Ponce.
Celebrant: Revd Ivor Ever.

'Ladies and gentlemen, this morning we're going to do something very daring: we're going to learn a new hymn.

Now I know that some of you don't like the idea of learning new hymns, but I feel we have to do it for the young people.

Now I know there aren't many young people at church this morning, but maybe if we were to learn some of these new tunes, that might bring them in.

So, I'm going to ask Mr Stevenson our organist ... (Arthur, that's you. No not just yet!) ... I'm going to ask Mr Stevenson our organist if he'll play through the tune.

Then the choir will try to sing the first verse.

After that, I'll give a signal for us all to stand up and we'll sing this new hymn from verse one to verse eight.

Now, if we don't quite get it this Sunday, not to worry. Not to worry. Because this is the hymn of the month and there are another four Sundays.'

The above would be copyright, were it not for the fact that similar words are heard all over the English-speaking world every Sunday.

But what follows (as you may have noticed if you flicked through the pages of this chapter) is not a quick way of getting musically illiterate people to read that system of ancient bar-codes otherwise known as musical notation. That's because teaching a congregation, as distinct from training a choir, doesn't depend on music. Church musicians should be aware that, for congregational singing, a basic understanding of psychology is much handier than a PhD in baroque appoggiaturas.

The following are not fixed rules, but proven guidelines. As in preaching, leading congregational song requires the leader to be aware that his or her personality is part of the process, and that what might work well for one animateur might not be suitable for another.

1. Forget everything that works with choirs

This includes grimacing if something goes wrong, referring to bar numbers and asking the people to sing *allargando ma non più mosso*. It also means dispensing with terms such as 'altos' and 'tenors', and it particularly means never pointing to a sector of the congregation and saying, 'I think one or two people over there are out of tune.' Such a ploy is guaranteed to silence the one in four in the area who in that instant will be reminded of the school music teacher or church music director who told them they couldn't sing.

Think less about being the knowledgeable musician and more about being the enthusiast who would like to get his or her friends to sing a really good song.

2. Believe in your own voice

It is the only one you have, and God is certainly not going to give you a transplant. It may not be of recording standard, but it is the means by which you will let other people know that any given song is singable.

I am blessed with a passable voice. One of my brothers has vocal cords that got him into the chorus of the Royal Opera, Covent Garden. I could never do his job and he probably couldn't do mine. If people heard him demonstrate a song, they might feel they could never emulate him; whereas I sometimes rasp and squeak and people think, 'Poor soul, we'd better give him a hand.'

If you already have a solo singing voice, and don't need to be told to believe in it, then learn to differentiate between using it for performance and for enabling purposes.

Years ago, the musician in Iona Abbey was a young woman called Mhairi Lawson. She has subsequently become an internationally famous exponent of early music, singing in opera houses throughout Europe and frequently broadcasting on BBC Radio. But if you heard her teaching a congregation, you would never imagine that her voice was any more than passable. There is no *bel canto*, no careful handling of the tessituras. Mhairi has the good sense and the humility to know that what is appropriate for a concert hall with an audience of two thousand is inappropriate for a congregation trying to learn a new tune.

So to the non-soloists: believe in your own voice as a great teaching tool. And to the gifted few: when teaching, sing much worse than your best.

3. Always teach at the right time

Perhaps the writer of Ecclesiastes didn't have enough manuscript, otherwise along with claiming there is 'a time to gather stones and a time to scatter them', he might have indicated that there is a time to teach and a time not to teach.

When I worked in London in the '70s, I used to go to an evangelical Anglican Church in Islington. Frequently after the entrance hymn, prayer and *Gloria*, the priest would invite 'Matthew and Helen to come forward and teach us some new choruses'.

So, from the back of this church a slightly abashed young couple would wander onto the chancel. He would take off his over-coat and scarf, unlock his guitar case and tune up, while his bride of recent months gazed at him adoringly. Then Matthew would make his way towards the microphone into which the priest had just spoken and either blow into it or say, 'Testing, testing.' As he did so, you could feel the dust of resentment billowing from the disconsolate congregation.

We would not sing. We did not want to sing. In fact we hated these songs, and we didn't like Matthew and Helen either. So there!!!!

Actually, the discontent had little to do with the music or Matthew and Helen. It was simply that the right thing was being done at the wrong time.

Public worship is a communal exercise in devotion to God, not the kind of occasion – particularly in a liturgical service – where the flow should be interrupted by teaching practice.

So when should we teach?

Always as people gather. Indeed if we believe that 'full, active and conscious participation' is essential for good liturgy, we should view the teaching of new material as part of the gathering rite in which the community discovers its identity as a singing assembly.

If people are going to offer God the gift of a shared song, there should be a practice in advance to ensure that what is offered is not faltering or half-hearted. If people learn the tune (and it is essentially the tune that needs taught, not the text) before they sing it during worship, it will be in their short-term memory and will be recalled easily either when it is played on an instrument or when the first verse is sung solo.

The proof of this is seen almost every evening in Iona Abbey where successive musicians (it is an annual post) take a few minutes before worship to teach new material to the ever-changing congregation. And because the prevailing wisdom is that the worship is primarily for God's pleasure and is a gift which should be offered with integrity, people always turn up for the short rehearsal.

I have a friend who has a similar procedure at weddings, which some might think are events least conducive to the teaching of songs. If Robert thinks either that the wedding hymns are unknown or that the congregation is unchurched, he'll stand in front of the assembly before the bride or groom appears and say something like:

I want to welcome you to this church today.

N.... and N.... will be delighted that so many have come for their wedding. This is a special day for them, and in planning it carefully they chose words and music which they felt would be very appropriate.

So that we can play our part and enable them to know we support them, I'm just going to sing the tune to one of the hymns and ask you to sing it back to me.

Then he sings the tune to 'la'; the congregation imitate him. He thanks them and disappears into the sacristy.

If God is worthy of our song, then it is worthwhile preparing it in the best way at the best time. And that is always in advance of its being offered in worship.

4. Only teach what you know

(The discerning reader may be feeling a little frustrated by now. So far, this chapter has been a bit like those recipe books which have long preambles about oven temperatures, the benefit of organic produce, and the need to keep surfaces clean, while all the time you just want to get your hands on the ingredients and start baking the cake. Now we're getting near the hands-on time.)

It may seem self-evident to say 'Only teach what you know.' But this is where a great deal of congregational teaching fails, as people who would never rehearse a praise band or a choir unprepared feel that because congregations just sing hymns, there's no need for preparation. Can you imagine what it would be like if a stand-up comedian, for whom rapport with the audience is stock-in-trade, turned up at a venue and began to read the punch lines of his or her jokes from a notepad? The audience would feel cheated, the jokes would fall flat.

It is the same with teaching a song. Just as our grandparents never read the text of the songs they taught us in childhood, but sang them to us face to face, that's exactly what we have to do when teaching a congregation. And this is where psychology comes in.

For example, imagine the following: A musician appears before a congregation, book in hand. He says he's going to teach them a new song. He's not sure of the pitch, so he goes back to the organ or guitar and finds the relevant note. Nose in book, he starts to sing the tune, makes a mistake in the fifth bar, says sorry and sings bar five again. After pathetically negotiating his way to the end of the tune, still without lifting his head, he says to the people, 'Now you do it.'

The result is a disaster. Subconsciously people think, 'This must be a difficult tune. He reads music and he can't sing it. How will we ever cope?'

But if, like Mhairi Lawson, she stands in front of the congregation without a note of music nearby, smiles at everyone and says, 'I'd just like us to learn this wee tune,' sings it effortlessly and invites people to copy what she has just done, then people know that it is attainable.

This, of course, presupposes that the musician will take the time to learn the tune in advance, with as much care as he or she would prepare an instrumental obligato to be broadcast live on radio. The principal difference with a congregational song, however, is that the musician has not only to have a feel for the complete melody, but should know its constituent phrases so that he or she can take it to bits and teach a little at a time.

There is, fortunately, a fail-safe test. If you can't sing the song you're going to teach while in the shower, don't teach it in the church. Most showers don't have waterproof screens behind which to conceal hymnbooks. The music we sing in the shower has to be in us. If we can sing it with gusto while soaping our armpits and washing our hair, we'll be able to do it on Sunday morning – as long as we keep our clothes on!

5. Teach without instruments

Again, this is simple psychology, often forgotten.

That certainly was the case in an Anglican cathedral in the south of England where diocesan choirs had gathered for a music day. At the final act of worship a new hymn was being sung, the words for which were printed in the bulletin. The organiser presumed that everyone would know the tune, *Engelberg*, but few did.

That became evident after one verse. To aid matters, the cathedral organist thought he'd encourage the congregation's confidence by beefing up the pedal line. So a loud 16ft bourdon was added. At verse three, he thought he'd try the mixtures to improve the vocal sound, but to no avail.

Eventually, the worship leader halted the hymn and asked if anyone could come to the microphone and sing the tune. A lady obliged, then invited the choristers to sing it back to her, after which the hymn was sung with confidence.

It is a difficult thing for many church musicians – organists, keyboard players, guitarists – to leave their instruments behind and simply use their voice. Some find this demeaning, some (erroneously) think it is unprofessional, some fear that it will diminish public appreciation of their instrumental skills.

But it has to happen if people are going to be taught a tune. For if the musician decides to play it on an instrument, the musically unconfident in the congregation will presume it must be a difficult tune. Otherwise the musician would just sing it.

In any case, if I play a new hymn or song on the piano or organ and have between four and six notes in any given chord, how is the melody to be heard? If I strum a guitar with six strings, where is the tune? And even if I play that most voice-like instrument the flute, how does the listener know which sung syllables go where?

All the time, my self-esteem (for which some might read arrogance) as an instrumentalist is looming more important than the need for the congregation to be taught properly.

Fortunately, salvation is at hand for the timorous. If the church musician, for whatever reason, does not feel able to sing the congregation's part to them, there may well be someone else in the vicinity who is an affable teacher.

In the worship group I used to lead, we normally had 18 people, of whom only a minority could read music. But some of the best teachers of new tunes were those who didn't know a minim from a doughnut.

If this all seems a bit alarming, worse is to come!

6. Teach tunes to 'la' unless the text is short

If, in deference to St Paul, we are going to sing with intelligence, we have to be comfortable with the words. But to sing the words, we must first be comfortable with the tune.

The tune is the prior issue, and la-laaing is a noble teaching art.

As regards the specifics, they are few. It is the simplest thing to take a melody, divide it into two, three or four bite-sized chunks, sing each one to 'la' and ask people to repeat what you've just sung. Then you ask them to hum the tune while you sing the whole melody to 'la' (for the virtues of humming see later) and finally get people to sing to 'la' with you.

This procedure does not require a diploma in voice production, just a little regression therapy. Simply remember what your grandmother did when you were small. She might not have known all the words to a catchy pop tune on the radio, but she would sing the words she knew and la-la those she didn't.

It may also be helpful to let people know the structure of the tune.

Let's take two examples and imagine we were teaching these well-known tunes for the first time.

Praise My Soul

Music: John Goss (1800–1880)

Praise My Soul (Lauda Anima) has three phrases. That is all people need to know. You sing them one at a time, then sing all three together.

Kingsfold

Music: melody from *English Country Songs*, 1893

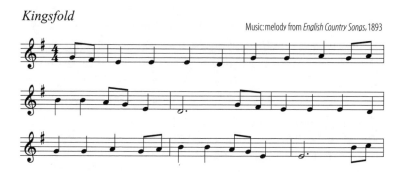

Kingsfold is, if anything, a little easier. You teach the first phrase, then tell people that the second is almost the same. You say that the third phrase is different and, when they have learned it, immediately get them to sing the last which they already know as the second.

If, however, the tune being taught is a repeated chant or worship song, where the words are easily memorised, there may be no need to employ the ubiquitous 'la'.

Be Still and Know

Music © 1988 WGRG, Iona Community

Cantor: v. 1   *Be still and know that I am God*

ALL: *AND THERE IS NONE BESIDE ME.*

                      BE STILL AND KNOW THAT I AM GOD,

                      AND THERE IS NONE BESIDE ME.

Cantor: v. 2   *I am the one who calls you my friends ...*

         v. 3   *I am the one whose love never fails ...*

         v. 4   *I am the one who says 'follow me' ...*

         v. 5   *Be still and know that I am God ...*

In the above song, it is sufficient to divide the melody into two phrases and teach by rote.

If new tunes are taught thus before worship begins, it will be enough for the melody to be played once, or for someone to sing the first verse, to enable the congregation to join the song.

7. Outline the tune in the air

(The discerning will now be convinced that the author is either mad or has just inhaled illegal smoking substances.)

There are schools of teaching, particularly in Eastern Europe, which employ hand signals for teaching children. While these are very effective, they rely on the children understanding the specialised sign language. What is described here is much more basic.

When I was involved in youth work, I realised that if I could get teenagers to look at me as I taught, they would learn more quickly. And I also realised that if I raised or lowered my arms indicating the approximate pitch of each note as I sang it, they learned more quickly yet.

Each of my colleagues uses this method to teach song to congregations, but each does it in a different way. So what is outlined here is a basic framework, some components of which will be more or less helpful to different people.

a) Begin by singing aloud a tune you know well. Without visualising the musical score, feel for where the tune rises and where it falls, for which notes are short and which notes are long.

Now try to sign the tune in the air with your hands as you sing it. Hold your hands flat, palms down and let them both go up or down together. Don't worry about making this a performance piece: it's just a basic exercise to enable the tune that is in your mind to become visible in the space in front of you.

b) You'll probably have discovered that if you make big gestures, you run out of space, or if you make small gestures, you can hardly tell the difference between the pitches of the notes.

What we have to do is to ensure that the signs you make are understandable to people who may be up to 30 yards away, yet they should not be so ostentatious that you'll need a ladder to indicate the high notes.

So, still singing the tune you've chosen, sing the lowest note and determine to sign its pitch somewhere well below your waist. Now sing the highest note and determine to sign it just above your head.

Your task is now to sign the whole tune within the parameters you have set.

c) So that we're all, so to speak, singing from the same hymnsheet, let's take *Twinkle, Twinkle, Little Star*. The tune has six notes, and none is far away from the others. Sign the first notes at waist level, the following change in pitch at eye level, and the third pitch at the top of your head. You should be able to sign the rest of the tune easily.

After this, try another easy nursery rhyme tune of your own choice.

d) Now, let's take the tune *New Britain* (*Amazing Grace*). It starts on its lowest note, so try signing the first phrase thus:

A-	midway thigh-knee
MA-	waist
ZI-	midway chest-waist
ING	waist
GRACE	midway chest-waist
HOW	navel
SWEET	waist
THE	groin
SOUND	midway thigh-knee

If you feel inclined, and even if you don't, try signing other longer songs in the air both to get used to the practice and to rid yourself of embarrassment. Gradually you'll feel like the Marcel Marceau of church music. But whatever you do, don't try to emulate the above example by writing instructions against syllables of words or your friends might think you're into a rare brand of tantric yoga.

This technique effected a minor triumph with a tall gangly boy who used to be in our worship group and who claimed he couldn't sing. But I noticed that if, in signing the parts for the basses, I stood near him, his head would move up and down taking his voice with it. A breakthrough came when I persuaded Neil to keep his head steady and just let his voice move. Two years later this 'tone deaf' teenager was accepted for Drama College and invited his friends to see a production in which he sang solo in front of a packed house.

The kind of liturgical aerobics described above are a great way to lose weight, not so much because of the manual exercise involved but more from the perspiration lost at first through sheer embarrassment.

Around the same time as Neil was learning to keep his head still, I was leading worship in a church in a town near Glasgow. I had taught several songs to the congregation using voice and hands only. Then one day I noticed a man from that church on the other side of the street. I waved over to him, but he didn't wave back – instead he signed some notes in the air. I was mortified. I was on the verge of deciding never to teach that way again when a colleague observed that he wouldn't have imitated me if the process wasn't working.

So, ever since, I have used the technique boldly and laughed at successive church and conference concerts where people have done convincing impersonations.

The more we do this, the more we will develop a personal vocabulary of signs ... how to indicate a repeated note, how to show a note should be held, even how to do an accidental and (as will be revealed later) how to sign two parts at the same time. But, for the moment, the basic practice of shaping the melody in the air by showing the different pitches is sufficient.

We may find ourselves bending knees to indicate lower notes, punching the air repeatedly when the same note is being repeated, and moving our hands at right angles to indicate a very small difference in pitch, as when an accidental appears in the music.

The important thing here is to feel that you are embodying the music. When tunes move from simply being notes remembered in the right sequence to music whose shape you can visibly demonstrate in the space in front of you, you're on the right track.

8. Never tell people the number

Otherwise, if you say, 'We're going to learn No. 346 this morning,' people will look up the hymn and, while you are diligently demonstrating the tune with hands and voice, the following type of conversation will be happening in different corners of the church:

> *He:*   *We've never sung this before.*
>
> *She:*   *No we've never.*
>
> *He:*   *What was that?*
>
> *She:*   *I just said No, we've never.*
>
> *He:*   *That's what I was saying as well.*
>
> *She:*   *Do you see who wrote these words?*

> *He:*   *Fred Kaan.*
>
> *She:*   *Is that not the name of the boy your niece is*
>   *marrying?*
>
> *He:*   *No. His name is Kant.*
>
> *She:*   *Can't what?*
>
> *He:*   *Pardon?*

For maximum attention when teaching the tune, don't tell people where the hymn or song may be found. It is a stage-by-stage process and the tune always comes before the text.

9. Always teach with expectation and encouragement

We only get from a congregation what we expect it to give. If we expect little, our whole demeanour will indicate as much. But if we can look relaxed, smile and clearly anticipate a good response, we will get it.

The good teacher does the job quickly, then the teacher gets out of the way to let the song be a common offering.

Sometimes it can be helpful to give a little information which might endear the words or music to the congregation. That might be to do with the reason for its composition, the country it comes from, a particularly insightful line in the text, or something interesting about the writer or composer.

But don't bore people with excessive information or so hyper-personalise it that people feel obliged to sing to please you rather than praise God. So out go introductions such as:

'This song is very special to me, and I feel blessed every time I sing it. Because I learned it on the day that my best friend's first baby cut her first tooth. And that was also three days before I was invited to sing at the Keep Sunday Special rally in Soho.'

Songs and hymns are not the self-referential property of those who teach them. There are other times for anecdote and testimony. When teaching, you should add to, never detract from, the worship.

So, to recapitulate, here are the basic guidelines. You might try committing them to memory or putting them to a well-known hymn tune:

1. Forget everything that works with choirs.
2. Believe in your own voice.
3. Teach at the right time.
4. Only teach what you know.
5. Teach without instruments.
6. Teach to 'la'.
7. Outline the shape of the tune in the air.
8. Never tell the number.
9. Teach with enthusiasm and expectation.

Inevitably, timorous beasties and flaw-detectors will have identified questions which demand an answer. The next chapter will deal with some of these. Then we might think about teaching congregations to sing four-part harmony without music.

(Now he's really off his head!)

Nailbitingly important issues for loose-fitting denture wearers

… questions and answers to clear up any confusion

1. What if all the people don't get the tune after I've taught it?

Don't worry.

At least don't worry if three quarters of the congregation know it. People learn tunes at different speeds, and the chances are that if the vast majority have learned it after your teaching, the others will lean on those who do know it and gradually fall into shape during the singing of the song in worship.

However, if the majority haven't got it, identify which phrase is causing the problem, go over it and then incorporate it in the whole tune, asking people to hum as you sing it and then to sing it aloud.

2. What's with this humming?

It is a remarkably under-rated way of helping people to learn.

The thing is that when we hum, we hear ourselves internally and the leader externally. This enables us to identify our mistakes and make the necessary adjustments.

Sometimes, when a tune feels as if it could be picked up very quickly, it might be sufficient to sing it to 'la' to the congregation, then ask them to hum it as you sing and sign it.

There are other occasions when humming can be a lovely enhancement during worship. For example, a choir or music group might hum in harmony an appropriate tune under a reading of scripture. Or – as occasionally happens in WGRG liturgies or in Iona Abbey – if people need time to move to the centre of the worship area for acts of healing or commitment, the preceding hymn might end with its tune being hummed while people move.

3. Should people never get staff notation in the teaching process?

Let me relate what happened at a conference of the National Association of Pastoral Musicians in Montana.

I had been asked to lead two similar workshops on congregational song with full-time and part-time church musicians. In the first workshop, I distributed no music and discovered that it was quite tough going to get people into the songs.

At the second workshop, I distributed music in advance, and people sang much better. The odd thing was that the music I distributed was not the music we sang. But perhaps the second group felt that by acknowledging their ability to read staff, I was according them a degree of respect.

So, it is possible to hand out music. But when teaching the

assembly, don't refer to it until the teaching is done. Otherwise some pedant who observes you putting a dotted rhythm where the music indicates a double-dotted rhythm will delight in drawing the mistake to your attention.

4. How many new songs should you teach at a time?

One or two, but not every Sunday. You have to win the confidence of the congregation and develop your own ability, so it is best to start with what is achievable.

Oh, people who have been to Iona Abbey or attended events run by my colleagues and myself will object that we always do more than that, which is true. But this happens when people have come expecting to learn new material. In a local congregation, not everyone comes expecting or even wanting to learn new songs. But if the first steps in congregational teaching are positive, confidence will develop in both the leader and the assembly.

And don't presume that the more affluent or educated congregations will be the keenest learners. In Glasgow a congregation of predominantly elderly people in a low-income part of the city outstrip their younger and more affluent counterparts in their zeal to learn new songs for worship.

When you begin to teach, it may be best to try your technique out on a group of friends or a small gathering rather than launch out on Christmas Eve or Easter Morning when the congregation is at its largest.

You will find, however, that different seasons and occasions increase the ease with which people learn. If there is a church anniversary coming up or some kind of special service, people may be keen to learn new music. If there is a visiting deputation from an overseas church, a hymn from their country might be enthusiastically learned in advance of their visit.

But for regular worship, don't teach something new every week, and don't teach more than one item until you feel confident in doing so and sense you have the congregation's support.

5. Should you sing a newly-learned song on the Sundays following?

Only if there's good reason.

Churches who have a liturgical service or who follow the Christian Year might want to sing the same *Kyrie* during, say, Advent or Lent. But if the new song is appropriate only for baptisms, don't include it next Sunday if the font is not going to be used. Instead, plan far enough in advance to ensure that it will get another singing, preferably within the next six months.

6. Shouldn't you get the choir to demonstrate the new song first?

Not if that is a ploy to avoid teaching the congregation directly.

Some musicians go to great lengths to get a new tune into the congregation's subconscious. The choir will sing it as an anthem one Sunday, an introit the next, and on the third, the Sunday before the congregation is 'introduced' to it, the organist will try to improvise on it during the offertory.

This is treating adults like children – no, worse than children, because children learn new songs very easily. It's displacement activity, trying to stave off the 'evil day'.

Because most choirs sing in harmony, it will be important to let them learn the harmony parts at their weekly practice. But on Sunday morning, they should simply be members of the congregation where teaching the tune is concerned.

What is very helpful is to have the choir, or a section of it, or a soloist, sing the first verse of the song when it is used in worship. But this first verse should be in unison. Remember, a congregation needs primarily to be reminded of the tune. If it is a five-verse text, it might be good to have the choir sing the penultimate verse on its own and then in harmony.

7. What if the congregation is resistant?

The key to dealing with resistance is understanding what's behind it.

This is not the place to go into the issue in detail. But these cryptic pointers might help. First, try to work out where people are coming from.

a) If people say, 'We've never done this before,' you might try the traditionalist approach:

One of the forgotten traditions of our church is the way in which during the nineteenth century there were congregational practices. They often lasted an hour. I'm sure our forebears would be delighted that we are following their example, but would possibly feel let down by the fact that it is only going to take three minutes.

b) If people say, 'I didn't come to church to learn new stuff,' try the ecclesiastical approach:

either

One of the great hopes of the Second Vatican Council was the 'full, active and conscious participation of the people in the liturgy'. So, when we learn new material we are fulfilling the dream of the blessed Pope John 23rd.

or

One great recovery of the Reformation was the right of the people to sing in worship. I'm sure if John Calvin were here today, he'd be cheering us on.

or

Methodists sing their faith. And our faith is not a static thing. It moves. So does hymnody. Wesley made it quite clear that singing was a way to learn theology. And because our understanding of God is always increasing, we need new songs to fix new insights in our minds.

Adapt or improvise according to the denomination.

c) If resistance is on a biblical basis, then:

either

Friends, we are commanded by God in the psalms to sing a new song for the Lord. It is that precise scriptural mandate which we are fulfilling because we are Bible-believing Christians.

or

In the Book of Revelation (Apocalypse), St John the Divine gives us a vision of heaven where those invited to the wedding feast of the Lamb are singing a new song. If that lies ahead for us in heaven, let us enthusiastically engage in the practice on earth.

d) If some people think it is just plain unnecessary:

Supposing we were going to spend an hour with Her Majesty the Queen. What would we do? We would brush our shoes, choose our clothes carefully, polish up our etiquette and think of what might be good subjects for conversation.

So, if we are going to spend an hour in the presence of the King of Kings, does God not deserve a little by way of preparation?

e) We've got enough songs already! We don't need any more!

Imagine you had been married for 20 years and you, as the wife, were given the same box of chocolates (candies)

by your husband every Friday for the rest of your life.
Would you see this as a sign of enduring love or a lack of
imagination?

Or, if after 20 years of marriage you were still saying to
each other the things you had said on your wedding night:

> *He: What I love about you, Jill, is your hour-glass*
> *figure.*
> *She: What I love about you, Dan, is your gorgeous*
> *curly hair.*

Would such terms of endearment be a sign of a healthy
relationship as she showed evidence of middle-age
spread, and he became as bald as a coot? So the way we
relate to God and the words we use should reflect the
changes in us and the world around us.

However, all these ripostes will fall flat on their face if the reason
for the resistance to new music is that we who introduce it are
either patronising, dull, constantly self-referential or ill-prepared. If
we are the problem, all the smart answers won't convince a soul.

8. What if the organist won't play new songs and the minister is reticent to choose them?

An incredible amount of unnecessary resistance and side-taking
could be eliminated if musicians and pastors cooperated as
colleagues rather than suspected each other as rivals.

The issue is too big to deal with here, but the 'professionals' have to get it into their heads that they are not employed to preserve their dignity or their idiosyncratic musical taste at whatever the cost; they are there to enable the worship of God's people. One individual's personal taste cannot be the final arbiter in the choice of words and music. To make it so would be to abuse liturgical power. It is necessary to consider what is worthy of God, what is suitable for the venue and what can be sung by the people.

So any priest who insists that the psalms should be intoned the way they were in his seminary is just not living in the real world. Nor is any musician who tries to apply the standards of the cathedral in whose choir he once sang to a church in a public housing area where Johnny Cash is better known than Gerald Finzi.

9. Can everyone teach?

If you can teach a child a song by singing it, you can do the same with a congregation. The best teachers, as indicated before, are not necessarily the most qualified musicians. They are those who, for a moment, can become the grandmother teaching her grandchildren a song she loves.

Advanced trapeze technique for beginners

… tricks of the trade for willing apprentices

My Wild Goose colleagues and I frequently teach short songs in three- or four-part harmony. Sometimes two or three of us will take a part each, teach it separately, then bring the parts together. But sometimes, one of us will teach all four parts. This mystifies observers unnecessarily. It is not a charismatic gift, but a learned skill.

As indicated above, people from other nations carry in them the ability to sing bass, tenor, alto and soprano lines simply because as children they heard various adults sing these different parts in the home as much as in the church. For them to differentiate between the four voices and memorise the parts is a natural activity. It is Europeans who find it strange. They tend to listen for the tune alone.

Years ago, I worked with Patrick Matsikenyiri, the great Methodist song-leader from Zimbabwe. At that time, Patrick could not read or write music, but he had composed a great deal and asked if I would transcribe one of his songs.

Having done so, I was surprised at what seemed like an odd chord towards the end of his song. It had E in the bass, D# in the tenor, G# in the alto and B in the soprano. I brought it to his attention, telling him that the bass and tenor were a major seventh apart and that constituted a clash; did he intend it?

'My dear John,' he replied, 'if you know the history of my country, you will know that we have had to deal with so much conflict that a little clash in the harmony will prove no difficulty to Zimbabweans.'

But rather than recount how others can remember and teach in harmony, let's look at some possibilities for everyone.

CANON LAWS

Begin not with a four-part song, but with a canon. This enables us to develop a sense of what it is like to have different people singing different things around us.

Begin, say, with the *Canon* by Thomas Tallis and, in advance of teaching the tune, remind people of the text of a long metre doxology such as:

> *Praise God from whom all blessings flow;*
> *praise God, all creatures here below;*
> *praise God above, you heavenly host;*
> *praise Father, Son, and Holy Ghost.*

When the text is secure, ask people to sing it to the tune opposite.

Before embarking on the canon, sing it through with everyone to ensure familiarity with the tune.

Tallis's Canon

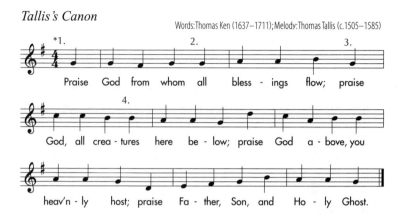

Words:Thomas Ken (1637–1711); Melody:Thomas Tallis (c.1505–1585)

Divide the congregation into four equal sections, naming them A, B, C and D.

Indicate that when we sing the song, we will sing it in unison twice, and then section A will begin, with subsequent sections following at one-bar intervals. You, as leader, should invite each section to begin by giving them a hand signal.

But how do you stop them?

The best way is to listen for what part A is singing. When the canon has been repeated a sufficient number of times, simply hold up a hand like a traffic policeman in front of section A, indicating that this group should stop when it reaches the end of the tune. Make a similar gesture to subsequent sections – then, so that the song ends robustly, invite everyone to sing it together for a final time.

The first attempt at this is always nerve-racking, but it works and the effect can be electric, especially if you don't take the canon too slowly.

In 2001, at the Greenbelt Festival in England, over ten thousand people sang Tallis's *Canon* in a slightly more syncopated rhythm than above, helped by drums to keep the tempo. It is best not to use harmonising instruments with a canon.

As an alternative to Tallis's *Canon*, you might try *Row, Row, Row the Boat* or even *Frère Jacques*, though how these could be used liturgically poses a bit of a problem. Perhaps during a French reading of the story of Jonah?

Having tried an old canon, try a new one. This can be sung to conclude prayer or as a recessional while people leave the church.

Celtic Amen

© WGRG, The Iona Community

A - men, a - men, al - le - lu - ia, a - men.

MIXED THREESOMES

The first three-part song I ever learned is a *Gloria* which allegedly goes back to the time when the Benedictines lived in Iona Abbey. The legend is that the *Gloria* was sung alternately by monks on boats leaving on a mission and their brothers on the shore sending them off. Reputedly, when the two groups could no longer hear each other, the mission had started for the one group and the house-work awaited the other.

Iona Gloria

Scots traditional © Copyright control

Glo - ri - a, Glo - ri - a, Glo - ri - a, in ex - cel - sis De - o.

This *Gloria* can be used with unequal voices; that is to say, simply divide the congregation into three clear sections and teach one part at a time. Start with the top part and teach it to the group farthest to your left or right. Then teach the second part to the group in the middle, and finally the lower part to the people on the other extreme.

You will realise that the first and second lines have similar contours, while the bottom line is a simpler affair. It is possible, therefore, to use one hand (the right if you are right-handed) to sign the upper and middle parts, and the other hand to sign the lower part. Try this at home in front of a mirror to ensure you feel comfortable with it.

When you have taught all three sections, build them up by starting with the upper part, then adding the middle, then the lower. Keep both hands moving for three or four singings, then simply use one hand to beat the time.

Slightly more rhythmic is the Peruvian *Gloria* (see overleaf), which again can be used for mixed unequal voices.

Here, every line has the same pattern. What makes this easy to teach is that it begins in unison and only breaks into harmony towards the end. So again divide the group into three sections and tell them in advance that when they come to the 'Alleluia! Amen', you will give each section two different notes on which to sing these words. Once given their notes, each section continues to sing as other sections join in, until you eventually indicate that all should stop.

Peruvian Gloria

© Copyright control

Sadly for some, there are relatively few canons or songs for mixed unequal voices compared to more conventional three- or four-part harmony. It is simply because most vocal music sounds best when the lower voices are singing lower notes and the higher voices are singing the tune. It wasn't always the case, as early Scottish Psalters and American Shape-Note manuals indicate. At one time the tune was in the tenor (a word which indicates that this voice holds the tune), but the girls won and ever since the boys have been consigned to the basement.

SEPARATED TRIPLETS

Here is a very easy *Alleluia* to sing in harmony with female voices taking the two upper parts and male voices the lower.

Duncan Alleluia

Music Norah Duncan IV © 1987, GIA Publications, Inc.

As before, divide the group geographically. Because I am right-handed and probably because I occasionally play the piano, I tend to prefer higher voices, male and female, to be to my right and lower voices to my left. This is not the most common choir formation, but we are not dealing with a choir, so perhaps it is a good corrective.

Teach the melody line to all the women and trebles on your right. Once they are holding it, which should only take two singings to confirm, teach the lower part to women and trebles on your left. Then teach the easy descending line to all the men throughout the congregation. Then build up the song one part at a time, in the order in which it was taught. Continue singing ad lib when all three parts are together.

The following song requires men to sing in two parts, and women and trebles to hold the tune.

Teach the tune first, but ask people to pay attention to the fourth time they sing 'come'. It is not the musically illiterate but often the musically confident who seem to think that the fourth 'come' should be at the same pitch as the second. If a few dominant musical personalities persist in singing what they think should be the right notes, it throws the crowd. So, to correct them on this and other occasions when the cognoscenti want to have their way, you might say,

'I want to correct one small error which only those who are used to reading music normally make.'

It will do you no end of good in the eyes of the non-readers to take their musical superiors down a peg.

Once the tune is correctly sung, divide the men into two groups.

Come All You People

Melody + Shona: Alexander Gondo, Zimbabwe
Transcription + English paraphrase: I-to Loh © 1986 WCC and the Asian Institute for Liturgy and Music
Arrangement © WGRG, Iona Community

Using one hand, teach the upper men's part to one section, noting that it is very similar to the tune. Then, with the other hand, teach the bottom, simpler, part and – to save anyone from the fear that they are cursing in a foreign language – assure them that the word 'Ahom' is a term of reverence, as used in the presence of a king.

When all three parts have been learned, begin working from the top down:

1st time :	Women
2nd :	Women plus upper men
3rd :	Women, upper and lower men.

When the three parts are comfortably established, sing the descant part yourself – whether you are male or female – or assign it to someone else.

Sadly – as with canons – there is not a superabundance of straightforward three-part short songs. But if you have developed confidence in working in three parts, progressing to four is not such a huge leap.

FORE AND OFT

The procedure is exactly the same as for the three-part songs. You divide the group into two main sections, and then deal with female/treble and male voices in each. But, to set it in concrete, let's take the following song:

Behold the Lamb of God

Music © 1995 WGRG, Iona Community

Be - hold the Lamb of God, be - hold the Lamb— of God.— He

Be - hold the Lamb, the Lamb of God. He

This song is easy to begin with because it consists of four bars of music which are repeated, and it has a two-note bottom line for men.

Teach as follows:

- Upper women's part
- Lower women's part
- Upper men's part
- Lower men's part

Then build up the song in exactly the same order as you taught it. A short-cut is to tell the lower men to keep singing after they have learned their part and bring the other three voices in over them.

Note that if you have started in a key too low for the 2nd men's part to feel comfortable with, you may want to raise the pitch a note or two before singing it in four-part harmony.

A slightly more complex song is this:

Dona Nobis Pacem

Music © 1995 WGRG, Iona Community

Exactly the same process pertains as regards the teaching. The main difference is that no two lines imitate each other.

BUT ... BUT ... BUT ...

... and that's basically it, except that there are probably a hundred questions which need to be asked and answered. So let's choose the best ones:

1. How can I teach four parts if I don't know them all?

You can't. So don't try. As with teaching a tune to an assembly, you have to know all the notes and sing them without recourse to music. That goes for the bass line as much as the tune in the soprano. Of course, it's helpful to have the book near you, but your confidence has to be in the internalised music rather than in the notes on the page.

There is, of course, a corporate alternative to which I referred earlier, and that is to share the teaching, with either two people teaching two parts each or four teaching one part each.

We have done this for years at a large open-air festival in England when there may be up to two thousand people present for a singing session, often sitting in the grandstand of a racecourse. We simply designate each of the voice parts to different people, who stand facing their charges and sign the music oblivious to what others around them are doing.

2. Should I get all the men to sit together?

Not necessarily. It very much depends on local circumstances. If, for example, you are teaching at a family service, it might be disruptive to force dad-with-the-baby to sit four yards away from mum. If it's an easily sung chant, there may be no need. But if the whole time together is going to be taken up with congregational part-singing, it would be helpful to rearrange the participants.

3. Does this technique work for everything in four-part harmony?

No, unless you are a black South African singing in the Imolanji Kantu Choir in Soweto. I wouldn't try teaching the *Hallelujah Chorus* by rote. Nor would it work for many 20th-century four-part hymn tunes where the harmony may be more chromatic or dissonant than in tunes from the 18th & 19th centuries.

It works best for many congregational songs from sub-Saharan Africa, Taizé chants and other short songs such as those written or popularised by the Iona Community's Wild Goose Resource Group.

4. When should I teach this type of music and for how long are short songs sung?

As with melody-line-only tunes, teach the harmony items before worship begins. Give people advance notice that when they come to be sung in the service, you will bring in the parts in the order in which they were taught and rehearsed.

When some short songs such as the *Glorias* get into the memory of a congregation, people may well begin to sing in harmony immediately. To start a song, simply sing the first bar or two of the tune to 'la'. This lets people know the pitch and the speed.

As regards the duration of singing, that very much depends on the use of the song. A gathering song such as *Come All You People* might be sung repeatedly until the congregation has gathered or the procession (if there is one) has made its way to the altar. *Dona Nobis Pacem*, if it is to be interspersed between prayers for peace, may be sung twice at the beginning to establish it, then once between petitions. *(See also the reference to short songs on pp106–107.)*

5. How do I find the right key?

I don't have perfect pitch, nor do I have relative pitch. I am the proud possessor of a third genus – appropriate pitch. In other words, I try to find a key which is suitable for the group I'm working with. Musically sophisticated congregations such as those of the Mennonite Church in the USA will sometimes soar effortlessly to a high F#. More timorous mortals, a.k.a. Scottish Presbyterians, tend to avoid anything above Eb. So, when teaching, as distinct from leading during worship, I may take the tune down a tone or two to let the higher women and men feel comfortable with their part. This may subsequently require a return to the written key after rehearsal if the adjustment in pitch compromises the lower voices.

Such a practice frustrates perfect-pitchers and choir members, who can't cope with a shifting or shifty doh. But the majority of people find such a process easy to handle.

When it comes to use in worship, it is best to get the note discreetly from a pitch pipe or have it played on an instrument. But ensure that you get what you need.

For example, if the tune is in A but the first note is E, it might be better to get the latter. However, if you are going to start people in harmony, where every part begins on a different note, it might be best to have the whole chord played and assign appropriate notes to each section.

What is true for many people is that, when you lead frequently, there are some tunes which you will always start in the right key. That's why the African-American women's group Sweet

Honey in the Rock doesn't rely on a pitch pipe. The music is so inside them that they simply know in which key to begin.

Similarly, I think of two friends who can always find F or G in their voices because they immediately remember a well-loved tune in either key and the pitch appears. This skill comes with self-confidence and familiarity. Until then, predetermine the appropriate key or use a pitch pipe.

I can't resist an anecdote of my first (of many) embarrassing musical experiences which shows that the right key is not always the best. It happened years ago when I was organist of a small historic parish in rural Ayrshire. This parish of Fenwick has a tune named after it, commonly called *Martyrdom*, and often set in the USA to *Father I Raise My Hands to Thee* and in Britain to *O For a Closer Walk With God*. The name *Martyrdom* alludes to the fact that the graveyard contains the highest number of memorials to 17th-century martyrs of the Scottish covenant of any such cemetery in Scotland.

The last detail is important because the event in question was a conventicle or gathering of people around a remote farm-house at Loch Goin in the Fenwick Moor, a place which had been the site of illegal gatherings of Presbyterians in the bad old days when Episcopalianism was making a bid for supremacy. A museum dedicated to the Covenanters was being opened and the service of celebration involved unaccompanied singing, as had been the necessary custom in open-air services in the past.

The tunes were all well-loved Scottish metrical psalm tunes and as I, aged 17, prepared to be the precentor, I was adamant that I would get the pitch right. Fenwick was not replete with pitch pipes.

But I knew my voice well enough to find G, which was the lowest note I could sing.

Psalm 103, verses 1 –5, to the tune *Coleshill* proved to be the offending article. The key was A minor, easy enough for me to establish. So I sang out the first phrase of the tune and conducted the congregation.

Come the end of verse two, the gracious Cameron Gibson, minister of the parish, said through the microphone, 'I don't know about you, John, but I'm finding this a wee bit high.' And he was right. Singing in the open air at a high altitude is very different from singing in a small and tightly packed church. So I took it down a tone and the transposition was enshrined for posterity, since a sound recording was made of the dedication service and deposited in the museum.

6. Do I continue to sign the pitches throughout the song?

No. Once everyone is established, simply beat the time with your arm. But if one part seems a bit deficient or weak, you may look directly at them and sign their line. Otherwise simply beat time and indicate any change in volume ad lib.

7. How is it possible to sign two lines at the same time?

How is it possible to play different things with your left hand, right hand and feet on the organ? It is not a natural talent but a developed skill, and it all starts with knowing the music well enough to be able to shape the melody and harmony lines in the air. But, like playing the piano with both hands, you cannot do it unless you practise it.

And the leader's practice should be done at home, not in the face of a worshipping congregation.

Nobody ever taught me this. I have simply had to learn it. But I know that it works not just because I do it myself, but because plenty of other people do it with equal ease and effectiveness.

However, it may be a skill which favours one sex more than the other.

Britta Snikkers was in charge of music for a diocese of the Swedish Church when I first met her. She invited me to lead a series of conferences on congregational song in different parts of the country. I was insistent that while I would speak in English, all other business, including announcements, should be done in Swedish.

Although I don't understand Swedish, I noticed that in her summing up of the first conference she made some reference to me which resulted in loud laughter. The same happened at the end of the second and third conferences. So I asked her what it was she had said that people had found so funny.

A little embarrassed (because Swedes tend to be polite to foreigners) she admitted: 'I just said that it amazed me how you could sing the tune with your mouth and conduct two other lines with your left and right hands. And you're just a man!'

8. But will people remember?

Yes, if they are taught well and they are not taught too much at the one time … and if you communicate that you believe they can do it.

The proof for all time surfaced in 1992 when a German television company had applied to broadcast the midnight Easter

Vigil service from Iona Abbey all over Europe.

Holy Week is very important on Iona. We try not to anticipate the events of Christ's passion and resurrection before they
happen, but rather to walk with him as the week unfolds. To
symbolise the devastation of the cross, no instrumental music is
played on Good Friday or Holy Saturday (until after midnight) and
the Abbey is draped in black cloth after the Maundy Thursday
eucharist. The broadcasting crew had shown sensitivity to the
season by draping their cameras in black on Good Friday and defer-
ring rehearsals until the Saturday.

At 7.00 pm, the residents and guests at the Abbey assembled
to rehearse the music for the vigil. They filled the choir, crossing
and half of the nave. Cameras and sound were positioned appropri-
ately, and during the rehearsal we learned this slightly more
complex setting of the text *Behold the Lamb of God*:

Behold the Lamb of God

Music © 1995 WGRG, Iona Community

As is evident, there is a canon between upper female and male voices, while the lower registers sing an *ostinato* to the text of the *Agnus Dei*. As distinct from usual practice, it was necessary to have the upper male and female voices on different sides of the Abbey to highlight the antiphonal effect. The chant was to be sung on a number of occasions between monologues depicting people in the Gospels who had witnessed the events of Jesus's passion. The chant, which was already known to several people, was quickly learned and we rehearsed it with the readers.

From 8.30 until 11.00 pm, people did their own thing, but we all assembled back in our seats at eleven o'clock for a final rehearsal and briefing. When I entered the Abbey it was clear that either piety or the presence of television cameras had induced around a hundred islanders and visitors to come to the midnight service. They were seated at the rear of the nave. Because nearly all the music would be new to them, I taught everything quickly, including the four-part chant.

When it came to the broadcast, being beamed live over Europe, something quite unforeseen happened.

We began the sequence of monologues which involved the singing of *Behold the Lamb of God*. At the end of the first reading, I gave out the notes, and conducted people through what was supposed to be a single singing. At the end of the chant, everyone who had been at the 7 o'clock rehearsal stopped, while the hundred newcomers at the back of the nave continued in perfect harmony for another cycle of 16 bars. None of these people had the music, all had learned the four parts just 40 minutes previously, yet by the grace of God and their own self-confidence they managed to sustain the song while panic reigned in the control room and at the podium.

PARENTHETICAL CAVEATS

One comment should be made in parenthesis:

Try to ascertain what is the politically correct term for people of the female sex. I have called this sector of humanity 'women' in some parts of the world and been told that they were not women but 'ladies'. In another place (or sometimes in the next town) I've called them ladies and been told that they are women. I've even tried 'girls' and had a female person in her thirties affirm that some of the company are old enough to be my grandmother; yet in groups of elderly females I have used the same term to much appreciation.

And what about children? If they have unbroken voices and are male, they have to sing along with some of the women/ladies/girls. 'Unbroken' can be a slightly awkward term, so it is best to say 'treble voices', which includes both boys and (young) girls.

And four caveats:

1) Try not to use the terms sopranos, altos, tenors, etc. That is fine for a choir, but not for a congregation. It also means that if you assign one section of the group to be 'sopranos', females in the other part who 'always get to sing the tune' will join in.

So, the best jargon might be Part 1 singers, Part 2 singers or, more colloquially, 'all the women (ladies/girls/trebles/) to my right and all the women etc. to my left.' Or you might say 'upper women and lower women' as long as no one takes that as a reference to social class or moral standing.

2) It is inevitable that even if you get the women/ladies jargon right, after teaching a line to a section of females and trebles, some men sitting in that particular area will sing along.

You have to stop that, otherwise the whole thing will fall apart. So do it with humour, saying, 'Now, now boys. Your time is coming!'

Or you might try a more anthropological approach:

'Friends, we don't have much difficulty with music in this place, but we do with sex. There are some men here who think they are women. If you are having difficulty in establishing your gender, ask someone next to you what they think you are.'

Or find more discreet words of your own.

3) Once you have taught the tune, gradually quieten your own voice, especially if you are using a microphone. Otherwise three things happen:

    a) people will rely on you and feel bereft when your voice suddenly stops.

    b) when singing together in parts, the dominance of your voice will unsettle those who are not singing your line.

    c) people of the same gender as yourself will begin to copy you even if, as a woman, you may be singing the tenor line.

4) When signing a song, don't have your fingers apart. It looks a bit like a penguin trying to fly and is very ungainly.

Typing for beginners

… odd things to do with the odd tune

... Nothing to do with keyboards, manual or electronic. More to do with recognising that when we sing, as when we read the Bible, we are confronted with a range of types or styles of material. And, in both cases, when we identify the type, that informs the way we read or sing the material.

The worst aspect of hymnals and song books (except when the songs are in alphabetical order and no two Christmas carols live next door to each other) is that each song is usually printed in the same way. In Britain, to the disdain of Americans, the words are normally on one page as a clear poem, with the music on the other. In the USA, to the disdain of the British, pew hymnals are invariably in four-part harmony with columns of syllables appearing between the treble and bass staves.

But both conventions share a placing of words and music from different centuries and in different styles next to each other, giving the impression that all the material is much the same. As a result, the songs tend to be sung and accompanied in similar ways.

As this is a book primarily about music, let's take the varieties of music first. If you want to play a game, cover the right hand column below and simply look at the names of tunes or, where there is no name, the first line. Try then to identify what type of tune each is. Write down your answers, remove the veil from the right hand column and either congratulate or commiserate with yourself.

Tune name (first line)	Type
Veni Creator Spiritus (Come, Holy Ghost, our souls inspire)	plainsong melody
Tallis's Canon (All praise to thee)	canon
Lobe den Herren (Praise to the Lord, the Almighty, the King of creation)	post-Reformation melody
Old 100th (All people that on earth do dwell)	metrical psalm tune
Sussex (On Christmas night all Christians sing)	English carol tune
Passion Chorale (O Sacred Head, sore wounded)	Lutheran chorale
Bunessan (Morning has broken)	Scottish folk tune
Holy Manna (For your generous providing	American folk hymn tune
Were You There (When They Crucified My Lord?)	Spiritual
Ode To Joy (Joyful, joyful, we adore thee)	symphonic derivative
Eventide (Abide with me)	c19th hymn tune

Tune name (first line)	Type
Sent by the Lord (Sent by the Lord am I)	Central American melody
Siyahamba (We Are Marching in the Light of God)	freedom song
Take, O Take Me (Take, O take me as I am)	repetitive chant
Gather Us In (Here in this place)	contemporary hymn tune
Shine, Jesus, Shine (Shine, Jesus, shine)	praise & worship tune
Ubi Caritas (Ubi caritas et amor/Taizé)	repetitive chant
Jerusalem (And did those feet in ancient time)	anthem
Verbum Supernum (Come, gracious Spirit, heavenly Dove)	plainsong melody

Here we are confronted with 15 very different tunes from very different places and with very different pedigrees. They cry out for their genres to be recognised and their music to be articulated with integrity. Otherwise, to misquote Henry Ford, 'You can have any tune you like as long as it's bland.'

The above categories are by no means exclusive. There are other genres and sub-genres. In the dullest of churches, under the least imaginative of musicians, they will be all be played the same way, typically either with organ diapason accompaniment or with every instrument in the praise band.

Such a practice shows the very lack of musicianship which church musicians would condemn in the concert hall. Nobody would accompany a serious performance of Handel's *Messiah* on piano accordion and kazoo; nor would the ever-ageing Rolling Stones be applauded if they appeared on stage to sing *Jumping Jack Flash* accompanied by a quartet of Elizabethan lutes.

Musical integrity – and it is a matter of integrity – requires that we respect the different types and styles of tune, and sing and/or accompany them in the best way, which sometimes might be in the original manner.

But rather than theorise, let's look at some of these tunes and think creatively. We'll take them in near to chronological order.

1. Veni Creator Spiritus

Melody: Plainsong metrical version, Mechlin, 1848. Text: Latin traditional

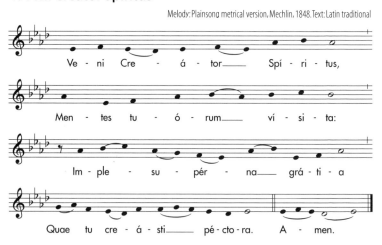

The melody may be sung to its original 9th-century Latin text or to the English translation by John Cosin (1594–1672) of which this is the first verse:

Come, Holy Ghost, our souls inspire,

and lighten with celestial fire;

thou the anointing spirit art,

who dost thy sevenfold gifts impart.

The melody is very old. It comes from the eighth century. It is an example of plainsong, often sung exclusively by monks and always in unison. So, to sing it well, abandon instrumental accompaniment. Have verse 1 sung in Latin by a solo male positioned not in the front of the church, but at the back or in a gallery, as this song is more of a prayer than a proclamation. Add unison male choir voices for verse 2, and have the whole assembly sing subsequent verses in unison and in English.

Similar popular tunes from this vein are *VERBUM SUPERNUM (Come Gracious Spirit, Heavenly Dove)* and *VENI IMMANUEL (O Come, O Come, Immanuel).* These can be sung in exactly the same way, though with *VENI IMMANUEL* there is a chorus (for which see later).

2. Tallis's Canon

Melody: Thomas Tallis (c.1505–1585), Ravenscroft's *Psalmes*, 1621

The next datable tune (though not necessarily older than items 3–7) comes from an English composer, Thomas Tallis. It appears in an English Psalm book in 1621 and has most recently been allied to a text by Ruth Duck:

The following is a suggestion for using the text:

v. 1   solo voice to give pitch and speed;

v. 2   unison voices;

v. 3   sing as a canon, with cantor/leader bringing in different sectors of the congregation who have been warned in advance that this will happen;

last v. sing in harmony after the canon has finished in the penultimate verse.

NB When singing such songs unaccompanied, there is no need to slow down at the end of a verse. Keep the tempo going.

3. Lobe Den Herren

Melody: from *Praxis Pietas Melica*, 1668

This tune dates from at least the mid 17th century. It has been associated with the text 'Lobe den herren den machtig Konig der Ehren' by Joachim Neander since 1680. It appears with variants in different manuscripts. This may indicate that it was not a tune composed for worship; it may have had more pedestrian origins. Played by a whistle on its own, it does make for a rather attractive waltz melody.

The possibility – as with other longer tunes associated with the post-Reformation church in Germany, Switzerland and France – is that it began life as a folk or dance tune, but through harmonisation was slowed down and made churchy. Most congregations sing this tune with pauses where there should be none and a total lack of any sense of three beats in the bar.

It might therefore be worthwhile forgetting about the harmony lines, and singing it in unison accompanied by flute and drum, allowing a vaguely mediaeval tone to enable the tune to dance.

A similar tune in this vein is *Geneva 42*, elsewhere known as *Psalm 42* after the psalm text to which it was set. It is now commonly associated with variants of the text, 'Comfort, comfort ye my people.'

Geneva 42

When I first heard this, it being was sung at something like 10 beats per minute in a church in Amsterdam with thick harmony clogging the airwaves. But remove the harmony and play it on flute or piccolo and the melody begins to dance. And to those who protest that the tune is not regular enough for a dance, the rejoinder has to be made that mediaeval Europe, like 21st-century Ghana, had a range of dances which were not as predictable in rhythm as a waltz or quickstep, but were easily enjoyed because people moved their limbs rather than their brains.

4. Old 100th

All People That On Earth Do Dwell

Melody: from *Genevan Psalter*, 1551

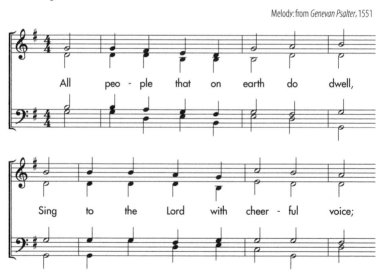

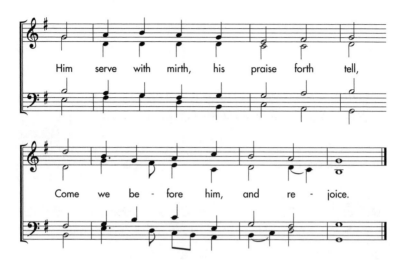

If we can't date *Lobe Den Herren* but can conjecture that it might have been a pre-Reformation tune, the same may be said for *Old 100th*. The melody comes from the *Genevan Psalter* of 1551; the harmony commonly sung appears later. It is one of a number of Genevan psalm melodies which, in their time, were emulated by similar long and common metre tunes from France, Germany, England, Ireland, Scotland and other nations.

Such melodies tend to be anaemic in their rhythm and sometimes in their tune. The reformers in some countries wanted to ensure that nothing inside the church sounded like anything outside and Scotland at one time sang tunes which now would encourage more yawning than believing. But occasionally we find in tunes such as *St Anne, Martyrs, London New, York* etc. robust melodies intended for a capella singing, especially in those countries affected by the Protestant Reformation which discouraged musical accompaniment.

So, we might want to sing this tune in unison for at least three verses. All may sing verse 1, women on 2, men on 3 and all, breaking into harmony, might sing verse 4. I encourage the harmony verse to be at the end as it tends to slow down a tune. But as distinct from *Lobe Den Herren*, no flute or drum.

5. Sussex Carol ...

Melody: English traditional

Like psalm tunes, carol tunes cannot be tied to a particular decade. *On Christmas Night All Christians Sing* appears at the end of the 17th century, but the tune may have been in use before then. As with other materials from the English folk tradition, this tune was popularised for church use through the harmonisation of Ralph Vaughan Williams. But that does not determine its use for ever. Vaughan Williams was music editor for *The English Hymnal*, a book intended primarily for Anglican churches, most of which had pipe organs, even in rural areas. Thus many such tunes were arranged by Vaughan Williams with organ accompaniment in mind.

But there is an older carol-singing tradition, recently represented on some recordings which feature Maddy Prior, where a couthy country sound supplants the perfect intonation of a cathedral choir, and diapason surrenders to a mixed bag of strings and whistles.

For, indeed, in 18th- & 19th-century Anglicanism and Methodism, as Thomas Hardy's novels attest, there were some churches which had West Gallery choirs, in effect instrumental ensembles in which local villagers took part, a bit like the English equivalent of Mexican Mariachi bands. The dominant sound would have been flutes, oboes, serpents and sackbuts – for which read saxophone and bassoon. There would also be strings in some churches and the harmony would be fairly crude.

So, a capella singing is one possibility, sharing the verse between voices with all singing the chorus. If there is accompaniment, let the emphasis be on the highest and lowest parts – say fiddles and flutes with a cello or bassoon.

Suitable for similar treatment, though coming from different periods, are songs and carols such as:

God Rest Ye Merry Gentlemen
Lulla Lullaye Thou Little Tiny Child
When Humble Shepherds Watched Their Flocks
The Holly and the Ivy
The First Nowell

6. Passion Chorale

Melody: Traditional secular melody,
from Hans Leo Hassler's *Lustgarten Neuer Teutscher Gesang*, 1601

Again, we cannot date this tune, but we know that in 1613 it moved from being a secular melody, which some would claim was a tavern song, to become a vehicle for religious texts, most notably *O Sacred Head Sore Wounded*.

It appealed to Bach so much that in the *St Matthew Passion* he uses it five times, and it is typical of other similar tunes which the Lutheran tradition adopted after the Reformation and which church composers adapted and harmonised.

There are therefore two legitimate ways of singing it.

The first, and older, would be to play it on the guitar in 3/4 tempo. That might sound a bit bizarre, but it would be to revert to a rhythm and an instrument (the lute was forerunner to the guitar) more in keeping with its origins. Indeed, we might remember that another well-known German tune, *Stille Nacht*, was originally intended for strumming rather than playing.

Other chorales can similarly be taken back to their original melody, stripped of successive harmonisations and played with very simple accompaniments to unison singing.

The second way is to revel in the magnificent harmonisations which Bach made of this and many other chorales. They are too important only to be played on the organ. They have to be sung – or at least some verses of them – by a choir which can allow every detail of the intricate passing notes to be sounded. Better still, preface or follow the hymn with an organ improvisation on the chorale melody. Or – as is common in Holland and Scandinavia – have an organ interlude between the penultimate and last verse.

7. Bunessan

Melody: Scots Gaelic traditional

Why should the tune to *Morning Has Broken*, a song popularised by Cat Stevens (or, as he is currently known, Yusuf Islam) in the seventies, be placed next to a German folk tune-cum-Lutheran chorale of uncertain but probable mediaeval vintage? For the simple reason that the tune *Bunessan* was written neither by Cat Stevens nor by Eleanor Farjeon who wrote the popular text.

The tune is a Scottish folk melody which was written down in the early 18th century from the playing or singing of a wandering musician on the island of Mull. The transcription is in the library of the Duke of Argyll. It was matched to a Gaelic Christmas carol text written by Mary MacDonald, a woman from the same island.

So, if this is a Scottish folk tune, how best should it be accompanied? With a fiddle or a flute playing the tune an octave higher than sung pitch.

The same question might be asked of a range of erstwhile Celtic or British folk tunes which have found their way into hymnals, tunes such as:

> *Kingsfold* (I heard the voice of Jesus say)
>
> *Slane* (Be Thou my vision)
>
> *Columcille* (No wind at the window)
>
> *O Waly Waly* ('Tis winter now)
>
> *Kelvingrove* (Will you come and follow me?)
>
> *Ar Hyd y Nos* (Through the love of God our saviour)
>
> *Bonnie George Campbell* (Blessing and honour)
>
> *Helmsley* (Lo! He comes in clouds descending)
>
> *Skye Boat Song* (Spirit of God, unseen as the wind)
>
> *St Patrick* (I bind unto myself today)
>
> *Clonmacnoise* (Christ be with me)

Take the first tune, *Kingsfold*, which is cousin if not sister to the Irish tune *The Star of the County Down*.

Kingsfold

Melody: from *English Country Songs*, 1893

Imagine yourself at a folk night in a public bar in Dublin with everyone drinking the national dark brown beverage of choice (not tea!). Imagine the compère comes to the microphone to ask us to put our hands together and welcome Seumas O'Leary from Cork who's going to sing *The Star of the County Down*. Imagine, as Seumas makes his way to the podium, the bar doors swinging open as a three-manual pipe organ is wheeled in.

We might be rather puzzled. What is a pipe organ doing accompanying a folk song? Exactly! And if it doesn't happen in a folk club, why should it happen in church? Why should the liveliness, the rhythm, the homeliness of a melody whose contours have been honed by public singing need to be 'supported' by diapasons and salicionals?

As with *The Passion Chorale*, we should seek appropriate accompaniment, so that we can sing the tune with integrity. And in Ireland, as in other parts of the British Isles, fiddles, flutes, hand drums or bodhrans and guitars are better suited to this kind of tune. The harmony in most folk tunes changes only once or twice in the bar. That makes it suitable for accompaniment on chorded instruments, such as the guitar or accordion.

This is particularly important because, as distinct from more grandiose tunes, folk tunes encourage text writers to use more intimate or domestic vocabulary. While we might not imagine a word such as 'kitchen' or 'pig-farm' fitting easily with a noble melody such as *Praise My Soul*, we could with *Kingsfold*.

And, since Jesus spoke of both kitchens and pig-farms, it may be that in gentrifying folk tunes we actually prevent them from being the vehicles for texts which speak of humanity rather than divinity.

Take another Irish folk tune:

Slane

Melody: Irish traditional

Like some other Celtic tunes, this melody can be sung over a drone. The first time I had it sung this way was in a large English cathedral with a congregation of around four hundred. I asked all the men on one side to sing the E♭ below middle C, and all the men on the other to sing a B♭ below that. I encouraged them to breathe somewhere mid-line rather than at the line's end.

The women sang the first verse undergirded by the male drone, and for verse two the women held the drone while the men sang the melody. Unbelievably simple, but highly effective!

8. Holy Manna

Melody: American folk hymn melody, from *The Columbian Harmony*, 1825

This is a tune from the North American folk-hymn stable, a pentatonic melody which possibly had its origins in the British Isles. It can be harmonised with two chords; if too many more are used, it loses its verve.

So maybe this, and other tunes like it, are best not sung with guitar, for fear of monotony. Instead it could be sung a capella with melody instruments – flutes or fiddles – and a small drum to keep the beat. This is particularly important with tunes of folk origin. Many of them, like spirituals, were originally sung or played to accompany work. If that was manual work which required a regular rhythm, like scything or breaking stone or hauling on ropes, there would be no break in singing between verses. We should emulate this.

The tragedy of much keyboard accompaniment is that the pulse of a lively tune is lost as the organist slows the last three bars down and pauses to change combinations, or the pianist slows down and pauses because that's what he or she has heard when the tune was played on an organ.

Tunes of folk origin need a steady rhythm, otherwise they turn flabby.

9. Were You There?

Melody: African–American spiritual

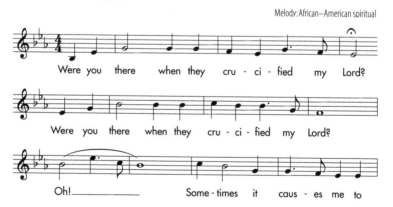

Were you there when they cru - ci - fied my Lord?

Were you there when they cru - ci - fied my Lord?

Oh!_____ Some - times it caus - es me to

Spirituals have been mentioned. They are akin to folk music because they were composed and sung by people at work and at worship. Sometimes, as on chain gangs, they were sung to enable people to do manual tasks together in safety, occasionally to tell news of potential escape from slavery in coded language ('The gospel train's a comin') and always to offer to God the pain or the joy of the singers.

Many spirituals have pentatonic melodies. That is to say they only draw on the notes doh, ray, me, soh, lah on the tonic sol-fa or sol-fege scale. *Were You There?* was possibly one such originally; now it has an added fah.

Pentatonic spirituals are inevitably strong and durable and should be sung slowly or quickly as the circumstance demands, but always with resolution and firmness. Take, for example, *Nobody Knows The Trouble I've Seen.* There is no prescribed tempo. As with other spirituals and many songs from sub-Saharan Africa, it is the occasion which determines the speed. If it is a sense of isolation that is being raised to God, the song is sung slowly. If it is the sureness of Jesus's attentiveness, it might be sung more robustly.

Certainly, in the case of *Were You There?* it is hard to imagine a speedy rendition; the subject matter is too ponderous. But many other spirituals allow for variety in tempo. And in singing them, voices in unison or spontaneous harmony are best.

Other popular spirituals include:

It's Me, O Lord, (Standin' in the Need of Prayer)
Swing Low, Sweet Chariot
There is a Balm in Gilead
My Lord, What a Morning
Calvary
Somebody Prayed for Me
Steal Away.

10. Ode to Joy

Words: Henry van Dyke (1852–1933)
Melody: Ludwig van Beethoven (1770–1827), from *Symphony No. 9*

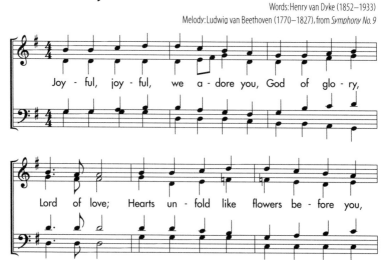

Like *Bunessan, Ode to Joy* was never written for the text it ended up with. The tune comes from Beethoven's *Symphony No. 9* and was originally accompanied by a full orchestra and sung in a complex arrangement by a substantial choir.

It is unlikely that such a rendering of the song could be achieved in a regular parish church. So, failing a nave and choir filled with double basses and trombones, the tune needs a good organ with a variety of tonal registers and volume.

The same is equally true of tunes such as *Jerusalem (And Did Those Feet in Ancient Time)* or *Thaxted (I Vow to Thee My Country)*.

Penny whistles and guitars or even pianos and clarinets won't do the trick. A big sound is needed from a big instrument.

11. Eventide

Words: Henry Francis Lyte (1793–1847); Music: William Henry Monk (1823–1889)

Now we come into the realm of what might be called 'standard' hymn tunes, often composed in the 19th century when the canon of hymnody was all but set in concrete. It is salutary to compare hymnals published in the 1880s with those published a century later. In many cases, the old stalwarts are still reproduced, the only difference being that in the 1880s often the majority of tune and text writers were still alive, while books of the mid-20th century tended to major in songs of the deceased.

The tune is dedicated to the text, *Abide With Me*. It is similar to hundreds of other Edwardian and Victorian tunes which are written in four-part harmony and often presume organ accompaniment, particularly when there are long notes to be sustained. The piano is therefore not the best accompanying instrument; and because the harmony tends to change more than twice in a bar, guitars are usually out.

Other tunes in this genre are too numerous to mention. But their prevalence has tended to encourage church musicians to believe that the way these tunes are accompanied should be applied to all congregational songs. I trust that I have by now managed to annihilate this assumption.

12. Sent By the Lord

Cuban traditional (attributed)
Translation © 1991 Jorge Maldonado
Arrangement © 1991 WGRG, Iona Community

Sent by the Lord am I; my hands are read - y now To
En - via-do soy de Dios, mi ma - no lis - ta es - tá Pa -

make the earth the place in which the king-dom comes. Sent
ra cons-truir con Él un mun - do fra - ter - nal. En -

by the Lord am I; my hands are read - y now To
via - do soy de Dios, mi ma - no lis - ta e - stá Pa -

make the earth the place in which the king-dom comes. The
ra cons-truir con Él un mun - do fra - ter - nal. Los

an - gels can - not change a world of hurt and pain In -
án - ge - les no son en - via - dos a cam - biar Un

to a world of love, of jus - tice and of peace. The
mun - do de do - lor en un mun - do de paz; Me

task is mine to do, to set it real - ly free. Oh,
ha to - ca - do a mí ha - cer lo real - i - dad; A -

help me to o - bey; help me to do your will.
yu - da - me se - ñor a ha - cer tu vo - lu - tad.

Here we have the first of two examples of contemporary songs from the non-Western world. For a long time (for most of us it was until the mid-eighties) the West was led to believe that the only Christian song from outside Western Christendom was *Kum Ba Ya**. It was variously ascribed to Africa, Asia or South America as if these were countries rather than continents. Now we know better. The Holy Spirit has been inspiring music in the South for as long as, if not longer than, in the North. It's just that Western Christians, especially those who believe that all good church music ended with the death of Palestrina, have been reticent to admit that they could discover anything worthwhile in foreign cultures.

Indeed, it would be fair to say that some missionary orders and agencies were wont, in the past, to demonise the music indigenous to the people in whose lands they were evangelising. I have had both Mozambiquan and Argentinian musicians in my home who spoke of how their ancestors were told that the drum (in Mozambique) and the guitar (in Argentina) were instruments of the devil.

How odd that the devil should change his favourite instrument from one side of the Atlantic to the other, and how odd that the demonised instruments – or at least their predecessors – are both mentioned in the psalms, unlike the presumed instrument of heaven's choice, the pipe organ.

Arguments rage at times about whether it is appropriate for us people in Europe and north America to sing songs from the Latin

---

*In January 2007, a businessman from Mansfield, England, said that he had visited the town of Kum Ba Ya in Ecuador where the song (allegedly) originated.

American, Asian or African nations, although in previous generations there was no question about the appropriateness of prescribing for such peoples a good dose of English Victorian hymnody.

Certainly there have been voices from the developing world, not least the Taiwanese musicologist Dr I-to Loh, who is rightly scornful of Western attempts to domesticate songs from other cultures either by reharmonising in a limp 19th-century fashion or transposing what was meant for solo voice with specific instruments into keyboard accompaniment.

Sent By the Lord, like many other Hispanic songs, has a clear rhythmic impulse and fairly simple harmonic progressions. Keyboard accompaniment, even on a jazz piano, kills it. It needs guitar for both percussive and harmonic effect.

Slower Hispanic songs such as *When We Are Living* or *Lord, You Have Come to the Lakeside*, may be reasonably accompanied on piano, particularly if the pianist can fill out the chords, but this is second best to the acoustic guitar.

13. Siyahamba

South Africa, traditional

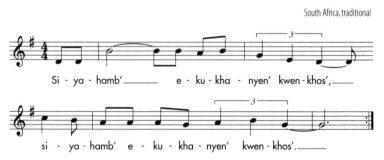

Si - ya - hamb' _____ e - ku - kha - nyen' kwen - khos', _____

si - ya - hamb' e - ku - kha - nyen' kwen - khos'. _____

Perhaps the most internationally famous of the songs of protest and praise sung by black South Africans during the years of apartheid, this song – as many others such as *Freedom is Coming*, *Akanamandla*, *Sizohamba Naye*, *Amen Siakudumisa* – is meant for open-air singing. Indeed some of these songs, including *Siyahamba*, were not meant for jovial praise meetings, but were sung defiantly as crowds marched to graveyards to bury their dead who had been massacred by agents of the state.

These songs come from black cultures where babies seem to emerge from the womb singing in four-part harmony. Many of the songs from South Africa, which my colleagues and I have transcribed, came from men and women who had no music reading skills, but who could sing soprano, alto, tenor or bass with equal ease at the drop of a hat.

The harmony is nearly always basic, favouring chords I, IV, V and VI, and the dynamism of the music is guaranteed, sometimes by syncopation but more often by simple counterpoint between the melody and other lines.

So, this music is not suited to keyboard or guitar accompaniment. Flutes and fiddles would be lost on it, but drums would help – as long as they are of the tom-tom and djembe variety rather than snares and cymbals.

And certainly, though they may be tempted to sing such songs, Western choirs tend to make a mess of music when they try to produce good vowel tone and precise breathing in material from cultures where consonants are sometimes more important than vowels, and vigorous singing of short phrases does not require pristine breath control.

Such songs are best sung unaccompanied except for drums.
Unless people know the song well, start with the melody, then add
the tenor, then alto and bass. The songs are usually sung continu-
ously as processionals or recessionals, so feel free to add or subtract
harmony lines in order to keep interest alive.

14. Take, O Take Me As I Am

Short songs like this have for long been used by the Taizé Community and more recently by the Wild Goose Resource Group and
the Iona Community. The four-part harmony may be sung by the
whole congregation or by those who read music, with a choir or
singing group sustaining the harmony throughout.

The purpose is to allow for meditation on the text or on what the text induces the singer to think about. So elaborate or fussy accompaniment is out, but keyboard or guitar are in, with the possibility of a melody instrument playing a simple descant.

As with some of the South African songs above, there is no prescribed number of times the song has to be sung. The occasion dictates it and to announce that we will sing '*Nada Te Turbe* five times' is to treat it as a strophic hymn which it certainly is not. However, it takes some time for congregations used to five-versed hymns to feel comfortable with shorter tunes and simple texts meant for meditation.

15. Gather Us In

Words and music: Marty Haugen © 1982, GIA Publications, Inc., USA

Gath - er us in— the blind and the lame;

Call to us now, and we shall a - wak - en,

We shall a - rise at the sound of our name.____

It is rather difficult to assign this kind of song to a precise category, other than contemporary. It is a strophic song. It has a regular metre. It does not have much by way of syncopation and its chord progression make it suitable for guitar and keyboard use.

But because, despite its structural similarities to conventional hymnody, it comes from an era and ethos partly in rebellion against the homogeneity of church music, it deserves to be treated to ensemble playing, with parts for a small group of instrumentalists derived from the keyboard harmony.

The great trick here, however, is to persuade instrumentalists not to play every bar in every verse. Changes in instrumentation enliven the singing. But just as some organists can be reluctant to change stops when accompanying hymns, some instrumentalists are under the illusion that by dint of having practised the sousaphone obligato, it should be played in every verse. It certainly should not!

16. Shine, Jesus, Shine

Words and music by Graham Kendrick
© 1987 Make Way Music. US admin. Music Services, Inc.

This is probably the best known of contemporary praise and worship songs from the English songwriter Graham Kendrick. At one time it was over-indulged in simply because it was so accessible and bright, in contrast to duller and less interesting tunes by other contemporary writers.

This, and many other tunes from similar stables, is unapologetically syncopated – something which sight-reading classically trained keyboard players find hard to represent.

Well, maybe they don't need to. Maybe when there is a song which the proficient but cautious church musician cannot bring alive by him/herself, somebody with a better feel for the populist style should be brought in. For truly it is as bad listening to a seasoned organist playing *Jubilate Everybody* on an undeniably non-percussive instrument as it is listening to *For All The Saints (Sine Nomine)* played on a guitar.

Musicianship is not about one person being able to do everything, or adapting what he or she cannot do to fit his or her skill level. It is about discerning how any given tune can best be articulated. This means that musicians should discern whether – given the tune, the text, the building, the musical resources – a hymn or song should be sung a capella or with accompaniment. They should ponder whether – if a text has a verse and chorus structure – one person might sing the verses and all respond with the chorus.

The discerning musician (of traditional or contemporary vintage) will be quick to identify whether she or he is best to accompany or whether someone else, more adept at a particular style, should be brought in.

When this happens, congregational song stops being the 'filler' between readings, prayers and liturgical action, but becomes a diverse phenomenon which enhances the liturgy and engages the people.

Morphing the muse

The hymns and songs we sing are more than tunes. If the truth were known, some tunes would never have seen the light of day had they not been composed to suit a particular text; while some others would never have come into common use had a text writer not been inspired by a particular melody. It is not a chicken-and-egg riddle as to which came first: in the majority of cases, it will have been the text.

Texts therefore have to be considered carefully when we think of how to sing a song. They are not all the same, and the structure or subject of the text might provide a clue to its best musical presentation.

As with the previous chapter, the categories here are not exhaustive; they are highlighted simply to increase our awareness of the differences in texts.

1. Amazing Grace

... perhaps one of the universally best known and best loved hymns. For a while, we who live in Scotland have believed that the tune was ours, simply because it could be played on the bagpipes. But the lack of any double stops (two similar notes being sounded in succession), and some historical evidence, suggest that this penta-tonic melody may well be of African-American origin.

But look at the text:

1. *Amazing grace! how sweet the sound*
    that saved a wretch like me!
    I once was lost, but now am found,
    was blind, but now I see.

2. *'Twas grace that taught my heart to fear,*
    and grace that fear relieved;
    how precious did that grace appear
    the hour I first believed!

3. *Through many dangers, toils and snares*
    I have already come;
    'tis grace has brought me safe thus far,
    and grace will lead me home.

4. *The Lord has promised good to me,*
    his word my hope secures;
    he will my shield and portion be
    as long as life endures.

John Newton (1725–1807)

Frequently sung as a communal song, this is actually a personal testimony. Quite apart from the first person singular (I) being used throughout the song, it is clearly an expression of personal and inti-mate regret – understandable since the text was written by a former slave-ship captain who had found both his Lord and a new sense of direction.

People who go to testimony meetings know that at such gatherings only one person speaks at a time. This, then, should inform how we sing the song. Here is one suggestion which presumes unaccompanied singing:

v. 1   Solo voice from the rear of the worship area;

v. 2   Everyone sings in unison to preserve the first-person feel of the text;

v. 3   Everyone sings in spontaneous harmony;

v. 4   Sing in four-part canon, each section of the congregation beginning a bar after the previous one.

Any congregation can do this. I write this with conviction as I once used this approach with the 'any' congregation. It happened to be Rosemary Presbyterian Church in Belfast. We began with *Amazing Grace*. I briefed the congregation as above and indicated that, come verse 4, we would sing in canon. I then said that we would sing – as Presbyterians had since the Reformation – unaccompanied. The look on some people's faces suggested that medical services might be needed to cope with the trauma. But they sang well and turned an otherwise regular hymn into a spiritual experience.

Go through the psalms (metrical version) as well as hymns and songs of personal devotion and many texts will suggest themselves as intimate songs of testimony which are never experienced as such if always sung loudly and in harmony because 'the congregation likes it that way'. Without prejudice to a congregation's expressed preferences, there is a pastoral dimension to song that is sometimes never experienced until the familiar is sung in a new way.

If I might take another similar instance from Belfast, it would be regarding the children's hymn *Jesus Loves Me*. I had suggested that this be sung as an adult hymn, that we would sing it slowly and unaccompanied and that it would begin with a solo voice. The impact was immediate and palpable. With the time given to reflect on the words because of the first (solo) verse and a slower tempo, it seemed as if doors into childhood were being opened as this text flooded the memory with fond associations from the past. Even the most straight-laced and dour of Protestant men were visibly moved.

2. Here I Am Lord

… is one of a smaller number of hymns written in a dialogical style. There are two voices in the text – God and the disciple:

> *I, the Lord of sea and sky,*
> *I have heard my people cry.*
> *All who dwell in dark and sin*
> *my hand will save.*
> *I, who made the stars of night,*
> *I will make their darkness bright.*
> *Who will bear my light to them?*
> *Whom shall I send?*

Here I am, Lord.

Is it I, Lord?

I have heard you calling in the night.

I will go, Lord, if you lead me.

I will hold your people in my heart.

Daniel L. Schutte (1947–) © OCP Publications,
5536 NE Hasalo, Portland, OR 97213, USA

Normally, in a dialogue, two people speak in turn, except it seems in the church where the one minute we are God and the next we are the responding disciple. Of course, one reason for this is that people like the tune so much that they want to sing it all, but in doing so we lose the impact of responding to the invitation of God.

The remedy is quite simple. Let one person sing the verse and everyone responds with the chorus.

A similar approach is suitable for Horatio Bonar's hymn, *I Heard the Voice of Jesus*:

I heard the voice of Jesus say,

'Come unto me and rest;

lay down, thou weary one, lay down

thy head upon my breast.'

I came to Jesus as I was,

so weary, worn and sad;

I found in him my resting place,

and he has made me glad.

Horatius N. Bonar (1808–1889)

Again there are two distinct voices as well as an element of testimony. When my colleagues and I use this hymn, we invariably get different solo voices to stand behind or at the side of the assembly and sing the first half of each verse, letting the assembly respond with the second half. This is particularly effective if the Scottish folk tune *The Rowan Tree* is employed, where the tune itself changes inflection half way through the melody.

3. Shepherd Me, O God

> *Shepherd me, O God,*
> *beyond my wants,*
> *beyond my fears,*
> *from death into life.*

> 1.   *God is my shepherd, so nothing shall I want,*
>   *I rest in the meadows of faithfulness and love,*
>   *I walk by the quiet waters of peace.*

Marty Haugen (1950) © 1986, GIA Publications, Inc., Chicago, IL, USA

Better known in North American churches, this is a responsorial psalm where the congregation is deliberately expected to sing only the antiphon or response. In most cases, the cantor introduces the response, immediately followed by the congregation. The assembly then listens as the cantor sings the verse and responds with the antiphon.

However, when this practice is used, the cantor should realise that she or he is not giving the performance of a lifetime.

Scripture is being shared and the cantor should back off from the microphone when the assembly is singing the response in order to maintain the dialogical effect.

Most Roman Catholics, some Anglicans/Episcopalians and even the odd Methodist or Presbyterian will be familiar with other psalms set in this style.

4. Let Us With a Gladsome Mind

1.   *Let us with a gladsome mind*
     praise the Lord for he is kind:
     FOR HIS MERCIES AYE ENDURE,
     EVER FAITHFUL, EVER SURE.

2.   *Let us blaze his name abroad,*
     for of gods he is the God, etc.

John Milton (1608–1674)

I used to hate this hymn with a vengeance. As a child I got bored with it. It seemed an endless number of verses with a repeated couplet tagged on every two lines.

What I did not then realise was that this is a paraphrase by John Milton of Psalm 136 replicating the style of the original Hebrew text. It has two lines of poetry then the refrain:

Give thanks to the God of gods;
his love endures forever.

This indicates that David, Asaph and whoever else contributed to the book of Psalms had something in common with the Rolling Stones, the Beatles and even Abba, not to mention a host of libretto writers of Hollywood musicals and folk singer/songwriters like Dylan and Baez.

The verse and chorus structure is as old as the hills. It requires one or two people to know the whole story or text, but only to sing a bit at a time. The chorus, sung by everyone, gives the soloist a break and lets her/him know that the audience want to hear more.

Like many mediaeval ballads, most pop songs of the 20th century had that basic structure. That meant that when the Rolling Stones came to Glasgow in 2004 to do their fifth or sixth last farewell tour, men and women with zimmer frames (strollers in North America) hobbled in but sprang to their feet when it came time to join in the chorus.

If the above is sung with one person taking the verses and everyone singing the chorus, the effect might be a bit tedious. Look at the text and note how verse 1 is an invitation, while subsequent verses are statements of fact. In which case, let a solo voice take verse 1, and then alternate the following verses between men and women with everyone singing the refrain.

More than that, let it be sung a capella with verses in unison and chorus in harmony. That will guarantee that whether the tune *Monkland* or *Herts* is used, it won't drag, but will keep its momentum.

It is salutary to go through any hymn- or songbook and identify how many songs have choruses. If a song's structure implies that not everyone will sing everything, don't feel compelled to do the opposite and make every congregational item uniform.

5. Praise, My Soul, the King of Heaven

1.　*Praise, my soul, the King of heaven;*
　　to his feet thy tribute bring;
　　ransomed, healed, restored, forgiven,
　　who like me his praise should sing?
　　Praise him! Praise him!
　　Praise him! Praise him!
　　Praise the everlasting King.

Henry Francis Lyte (1793–1847), from Psalm 103

No confessional intimacy here, no clear verse and chorus structure. Instead – as happens with many Victorian hymns – five verses of between four and eight lines. And not all of them have tunes as attractive as *Praise My Soul.*

So what do we do? Some people would simply omit a verse in the interests of brevity, but that sometimes spoils the argument of the text.

Maybe in such instances we can let the church in its singing do what Paul hoped for when he saw singing as a means of building up the body. To be enlightened or encouraged each of us needs to be mentored by another. We cannot do it all on our own.

So, in the song of the church, it is perfectly possible for different sections in the congregation to sing different verses of a song or hymn while others listen and follow the text. We thereby end up understanding the words far better than if we sang everything ourselves and became breathless with the sheer physical effort.

If Bach in his church cantatas could have parts sung by soloists, choir and congregation, so can we. Thus, *Praise My Soul* might be apportioned:

v. 1   ALL in unison.

v. 2   Choir in harmony.

v. 3   Women and trebles.

v. 4   Choir in harmony.

v. 5   ALL with an alternative harmonisation
        for accompaniment.

Apart from anything else, this allows choir and congregation to dialogue with each other, something which is not common. Or, if no choir is available, either a solo voice or children could sing the second and fourth verses.

Many church musicians baulk at the prospect of men in the congregation singing a verse on their own. But that apprehension has to be hit on the head. It is demeaning to men to expect them not to be able to sing.

One of my ministerial colleagues went to a new church near Glasgow, and decided in consultation with the director of music to have one Sunday per month where at least one of the songs would be shared among people according to age or gender.

He discovered subsequently when visiting in the parish that an amazing number of people, women especially, wanted to thank and encourage him for enabling the song of the people to come alive. Mention was made specifically of the verses sung by men in the congregation. For women, not only was it a singular delight to hear male voices, but it let their sons and grandsons know that singing was not an exclusively female activity.

A contemporary hymn such as Brian Wren's *Bring Many Names* is particularly enhanced by such a simple device as sharing the verses around the congregation, the more so since rather than being a continuous narrative each verse has a different thought which can be presented to the assembly by a different sub-section.

In most denominational hymnals, probably up to half the items could be sung in a similar fashion.

6. Amen Siakudumisa

> *Amen siakudumisa. Amen siakudumisa.*
> *Amen bawo. Amen bawo.*
> *Amen siakudumisa.*
>
> South African traditional

There is little to say about this which has not been covered in the section above dealing with African songs. But there is something which this shares with *Kyrie Eleison*, *Alleluia* and *Gloria in Excelsis* – it is in a language foreign to most Western worshippers.

So, if we are using a text from another culture in the indigenous language, it is always helpful to let people know what they are singing. We can no longer presume, in a post-modern society, that everyone knows what *Kyrie Eleison* means, let alone *Amen Siakudumisa*. So either when introducing the chant or when printing it in the brochure, give the English equivalent. (By the way, the Xhosa text means, 'Amen, praise the name of the Lord.')

To those who grimace at the mere thought of singing in a foreign language, two things might be said.

The first is that the church is a de facto international body. Not all Roman Catholics are Italian, nor are all Lutherans Swedish. We should be able to celebrate our internationality, and we can do that when occasionally we sing a song from another culture, using a language not our own. We sing Latin and Greek texts, because they link us with the Christians in the past; we sing Spanish or Xhosa because they join us to Christians in the worldwide church today.

Secondly, sometimes a phrase in a foreign language is much neater than the equivalent in our own tongue. If, for example, we were suddenly to drop dead would we prefer that our relatives were asked to give permission for our cadaver to be cut up or for us to have a post mortem?

As a prominent Roman Catholic musician in Chicago is wont to remind his colleagues: 'If you can say caffè latte, you can say Jubilate!'

* * * * *

This book is not conclusive, but you have to end somewhere.

It is the hope of the author that the foregoing chapters will have riled some people, affirmed others and amused or bemused all. If it were not that I passionately believe in the importance of congregational song, I would have written a much shorter manual with ten tips as to how to get it right.

But leading congregational song calls for more than technique. It depends primarily on the relationship which the musician forges with the assembled people and on his or her desire to enable sung texts to become meaningful experience.

Technical manuals cannot enable the development of either relationships or desire. Hence the previous pages have been full of anecdotes drawn from my own and other people's experience. But few if any of those whom I have cited are people who would claim to have great musical ability in an academic sense. Some of the best teachers of congregational song I work with are men and women who could not sight-read a hymn-tune on a keyboard, but that does not prevent their love of songs and of singing being the prime and winsome agent in the way they enthuse congregations.

And some of the most skilled musicians I am privileged to work with (as mentioned above) have become great teachers of congregational song because they set their professional instrumental or choral skills to the side and discovered how to get involved with the people.

For them, as for Jesus, the text undergirding the way they relate to God's people is:

'I did not come to call you servants, but friends.' John 15:15

God's worldwide Church

... some liturgical perspectives

PRIMARY CONDITIONING

It is 11.45 on a spring Sunday morning.

It is the late '50s somewhere in Presbyterian central Scotland, or Anglican Northumbria or the Methodist Dales. The primary Sunday school for children between 5 and 8 is almost over, but the offering has still to be taken. The pianist opens a red-covered book of child songs by Carey Bonner, and turns to a well-thumbed page. After four bars of introduction the children begin to sing:

> *Do you see this penny?*
> *It is brought by me*
> *for the little children*
> *far across the sea.*
> *Hurry, penny, quickly*
> *though you are so small;*
> *help to tell the heathen*
> *Jesus loves them all.*

As the children sing, they dip into their pockets for their missionary penny and, as they start to sing the song for a second time, they begin to file out to a table at the front of the hall. It has a white cloth over it, and in the middle is placed a cast iron model of the head and shoulders of a human being.

The figure has a red jacket, which matches his red lips. The rest of him, teeth apart, is black or brown. He is affectionately referred to by children and teachers alike as 'Black Sambo'. 'Sambo' has an arm and hand which is held, palm upwards just below his open mouth. One by one the children put their penny on his palm, twist his ear, and he swallows the penny.

> *Do you see this penny?*
> *It is brought by me*
> *for the little children*
> *far across the sea.*
> *Hurry, penny, quickly*
> *though you are so small;*
> *help to tell the heathen*
> *Jesus loves them all.*

This cameo of missionary commitment is but a reflection of what would have been happening in adult church assemblies throughout Britain in the immediate post-war period, when the spirit of triumph and victory, epitomised in the Festival of Britain, temporarily buttressed the notion that Britannia still ruled the waves and that – in ecclesiastical terms – the dark continents were still beholden to British missionary zeal. So it was that, without a second thought, adults could swell their voices in such sublime verses as:

Let the Indian, let the Negro,
let the rude barbarian see
that divine and glorious conquest
once obtained on Calvary
Let the Gospel, let the Gospel
loud resound from pole to pole.

or

Coming, coming, yes they are,
coming, coming from afar;
from the wild and scorching desert
Afric's sons of colour deep;
Jesus' love has drawn and won them,
at the cross they bow and weep.
Coming, coming, yes they are,
coming, coming from afar;
from the fields and crowded cities
China gathers to his feet;
in his love Shem's gentle children
now have found a safe retreat.

or

What though the spicy breezes
blow soft o'er Ceylon's isle,
though every prospect pleases
and man alone is vile;
in vain with lavish kindness,

the gifts of God are strown,

the heathen in his blindness

bows down to wood or stone.

or – to give a more balanced view –

If you cannot cross the ocean

and the heathen lands explore,

you can find the heathen nearer,

you can help them at your door.

Such pristine nuggets of religious verse – sung well into the '60s and '70s in some places – were not the products of post-war piety. They were written a century before, when the church's social conscience encouraged wordsmiths to produce tomes of verse dealing with two 19th-century socio-political realities – a high rate of child mortality caused by urbanisation and industrialisation, and the territorial expansion of the British Empire.

A world-view which saw whole continents tied to the apron strings of the United Kingdom, which presumed the English language to be the *lingua franca* for civilisation, and which imagined that evangelism in the Southern hemisphere was the duty and joy of the established churches in the North is epitomised in this delightful extract from *The Annals of the Poor*, published in 1893 and written by the Reverend Legh Richmond, late rector of Turvey, Bedfordshire. In the chapter entitled 'The Negro Servant', the Reverend Richmond begins by commenting:

If a map of the world, instead of being coloured, as is usual, with many gay and brilliant tints, in order to distinguish its various continents, kingdoms and islands from each other, were to be painted with darker or brighter hues correspon-ding with the spiritual character of the inhabitants, what a gloomy aspect would be presented, to the eye of the 'Christ-ian' geographer, by the greater portion of the habitable globe! How dark would be the shade thus cast over the larger districts of the vast continents of Asia and America! And what a mass of gloom would characterise the African quarter of the world!

The Reverend Richmond's tale of everyday countryfolk then goes on to describe his encounter with a man who was shipped as a slave from Africa to Jamaica, then to America and ultimately to the parish of Turvey in Bedfordshire, where he was brought to the attention of the Reverend Richmond who, for the first thirty pages, refers to him as 'my Negro disciple'.

William – for that is he – is desirous of baptism. After instruction by the Reverend Richmond, he is publicly examined regarding his life and belief in the company of rural parishioners, not in church but in one of their homes.

Among many questions, William is asked by the rector, 'How was any change brought about in you?' William replies:

'God let me be made slave by white men to do me goot.'
'How to do you good?'

'He take me from the land of darkness, Massa, and
bring me to de land of light.'

'Which do you call the land of light? The West
Indian Islands?'

'No Massa. America be de land of light to me; for
dere me first hear goot minister preach.'

The end of the public catechising sees William joining in a good old missionary ballad to which, for the special occasion of baptism, 'the following verses were added and sung by way of conclusion':

See a stranger comes to view,
though he's black, he's comely too,
comes to join the choirs above,
singing of redeeming love.

Welcome, Negro, welcome here,
banish doubt and banish fear;
you, who Christ's salvation prove,
praise and bless redeeming love.

A TWENTIETH-CENTURY OVERVIEW

To what purpose all this? – one might fairly ask.

The purpose is simply to illustrate where – as regards global faith – the churches have so recently been, and realistically rather than pessimistically to suggest that the colonial mindset which prevailed into the last quarter of the 20th century will not be eradicated overnight either on these or 'on heathen shores afar'.

Indeed the unchallenged sentiments of that late Victorian book, and of the missionary songs popular in the first half of the 20th century, may – in retrospect – be seen as contributory to the overt and covert racism still extant in 21st-century societies.

Those of my vintage and slightly younger may remember that well into the 1970s Saturday evenings on BBC television featured a highly popular programme which invariably included religious songs. This was not a Seventh Day Adventist *Songs of Praise*, but a show of musical entertainment which featured a dozen or so white men with faces blackened by theatrical make-up, singing and dancing with an equal number of white women, and offering the British public a diet of up-beat spirituals which had originally been sung by slaves in a chain gang, such as *Swing Low Sweet Chariot* and *Nobody Knows the Trouble I've Seen*. These alternated with more contemporary ditties from such well-known songwriters as Stephen Foster and Noel Coward.

Because I am convinced that people's beliefs are shaped more by what they see and sing than by what they hear, the effect of the missionary hymns, the penny-eating Black Sambos and the Saturday evening *Black and White Minstrels* broadcasts may linger long in the British religious psyche.

Its presence certainly became clear to my Wild Goose colleagues and me in the late '80s when we were asked to lead music at a large 'missionary gathering' in Glasgow. Some eight hundred supporters of foreign missions were there. When we attempted to introduce church songs from South Africa which we had previously taught the Communist Party to sing at anti-apartheid demonstrations, there was visible and audible resistance. It was not until the 'real mission praise' about the benighted heathen was sung that musical gusto reverberated through the assembly. And this despite the fact that as far back as 1910 an American clergyman called John Raleigh Mott was responsible for the famous Edinburgh Missionary Conference where he delivered what is generally accepted as a monumental address entitled *Towards a Larger Christ*. In this he encouraged a reorientation of global church thinking away from a hierarchical to a cooperative model.

The 1910 conference was a major precursor of the World Council of Churches and tolled – at least philosophically – the death knell of imperialist theology. But what is rehearsed at an international conference, or what is taught in a seminary, may take a century or two to permeate to the places where people are wont to sing of 'God's sun-kissed children'.

I mentioned above that the hesitancy to change the patronising relationship of the mission-sending to the mission-receiving churches was as prevalent on foreign shores as on our own. This is not so much a resistance to change or indigenisation in African, Asian or Southern American churches as the legacy of their theological and liturgical formation which cannot easily be shaken off.

Witness how in such vastly different places as Mozambique and Peru, the drum – common to the musical cultures of both lands – is only hesitatingly used in public worship. Why? Because missionaries in the last century made plain that the drum was an instrument of the devil. With that conviction in mind, pipe organs and harmoniums were shipped from Europe all around the globe.

Witness how in Argentina, where the music and rhythm of the tango is almost genetically compounded in the blood of the people, it was not until the 1980s that any Christian musician dared to use this native form of cultural expression in the liturgy of the church – and that simply because the European missionaries had pronounced negative judgement on such an art form.

Witness how, even in black Anglican South Africa, it was not perhaps until the consecration of Desmond Tutu, at which event a black choir sang *Amen Siakudumisa*, that the folk tunes, rhythms and hymns of the people were regarded as worthy for liturgical use in the 'established' churches. Until then the staple diet for congregational song had included the folk tunes of the British Isles as found articulating *Be Thou My Vision, I Heard the Voice of Jesus* and *Amazing Grace*, and the erstwhile sea-shanty tune redeemed by the text of *Lo He Comes in Clouds Descending*.

… And all this not so much because the peoples of the southern hemisphere had innate reservations about their indigenous cultures, but because they were so beholden to the teaching of Western evangelists and missionaries that they were reticent to fully inculturate and incarnate the Gospel in their own experience.

Six years ago, I was invited to Japan and, among other things, was stunned by the architecture of a church I worshipped in and the questions addressed to me by Japanese Protestant clergy.

The church – built around 10 years ago – exhibited few Japanese architectural features or devices. It had a central podium and pulpit on either side of which was a door – exactly the ground plan of a thousand British Methodist or Congregational churches. What was particularly unnerving was that neither of the doors led anywhere. They were simply affixed to the wall to resemble the architecture of the home churches of the European and American missionaries.

When it came to a lecture I gave to clergy about major shifts in liturgical practice, the questions were not so much to do with my theme as about the place of John Knox's Confession in the contemporary worship of the Church of Scotland. These prelates were quite taken aback when I said that probably only 5% of Scottish ministers would know that such a thing existed, and few if any of them would know where to find it. It certainly wasn't staple fare for public recitation Sunday by Sunday!

WINDS OF CHANGE

Having perhaps seemed fairly negative in my review so far, let me turn to the positives, and deal firstly with liturgical development in the nations we cautiously describe as developing, third world or Southern.

Undoubtedly, for many Southern cultures, the impulse towards indigenisation came with the documents of Vatican II in which the Roman church decided to loosen the worldwide stranglehold of the Vulgate, and Western forms of dress and liturgical practice.

It was not an overnight change, partly because there were no cohorts of Asian and African liturgists promulgating alternative strategies in advance of the Council's decision. Furthermore, there would be a significant number of National Councils of Bishops dominated by a Western mentality which would have severe reservations about empowering laity and clergy to indigenise celebrations of the Mass. But indigenisation has happened.

Thus, as Father Tom Kane, a Paulist priest and film-maker, has documented, one finds morning worship in Zairean convents danced by nuns in time to the pulse of the grinding of maize by village women. And in the Sunday Mass there is the occasional practice of men in tribal costume with spears and other artefacts dancing the liturgy.

Thus in India the celebrant no longer needs to stand behind a Western altar in a 20th-century toga, but may wear the dress of a native holy man and squat, cross-legged, behind a low table.

Thus in Hawaii (an autonomous nation taken over by the USA at the turn of the 19th century) Mass has an interesting range of local cultural resonances. When I last visited the Big Island, I was taken aback by the democratisation of the liturgy. The priest began by saying that he celebrated Mass on behalf of and with permission of the people. To symbolise that, he therefore wanted someone from the gathering to sit in the presider's chair (otherwise occupied by the priest or, on occasions when he visited, the Bishop). So a grey-haired 70-year-old Caucasian woman was invited up and she sat there smiling all through the Mass, as radiant as God.

When it came to the reading of the Gospel, the priest was aware that by regulations governing ritual, only the ordained servant should read it at Mass. But again – to involve the people and have their assent to his reading – all the while the congregation sang an Alleluia, he paraded the book of the Gospels through the church inviting people to touch it. When sufficient numbers had done so, and he felt he had the assent of the community, then he read.

Examples from Anglican or Methodist or other Protestant communities are not quite so abundant. Perhaps this is because – unlike the Roman Catholic Church – there is no global council that has authority to demand substantial changes in the practice of autonomous churches of the respective traditions.

Indeed, one of the concerns of many Christians in Central Africa and parts of Asia where American missionary activity is concentrated, is that native expressions of worship are sometimes eclipsed by the glitzy consumerist models made popular by certain representations of Western evangelism. At the present moment, a California-based broadcasting organisation called Trinity records evangelistic programmes in a Hollywood studio featuring the evangelical equivalents of more renowned secular Country & Western stars. Subscribers in the US are enabling these music broadcasts to be beamed over to sub-Saharan Africa in evident ignorance of the rich indigenous Christian musical cultures which do not need to be supplanted by trite commercial jingles.

But there are also, even in the Protestant camps, signs of renewal. Take, for example, a Lenten practice in some small independent Baptist churches in the Philippines. On Good Friday the congregation gather and sit around a Western crucifix on which is nailed to the wood a clearly Caucasian Jesus. The artefact will have been imported, or more probably donated, by foreign missionary agencies. When all are assembled, they begin to smash the icon to pieces, and then in groups they build a bamboo cross and make a clearly Asian rag-doll Jesus which they affix to the bamboo. Then they proceed with their devotion to the crucified saviour.

Asked why this practice takes place, pastor Nestor Bunda replied, 'We do it because we believe that Christ can only liberate the Filipino people when they liberate Christ from being the puppet of American religious imperialism.'

NORTHERN DEVELOPMENTS

Finally, let me return to northern shores.

To identify signs of a changed global consciousness in British churches is not as easy as when one is dealing with the churches in the South. This is true also for North America despite the incorporation of many Korean, Japanese, Mexican and Puerto Rican nationals into the North American churches. Rather than risk the adventure of developing liturgical practices which reflect the cultures present at worship, the trend is more towards letting foreign nationals have their own worship which might never impinge on that of the 'locals', or to have multicultural services which verge on the patronising.

But at least in the contemporary hymnals of the Catholic, Presbyterian, Methodist and Mennonite traditions in the USA there are representations of text and tune from the southern hemisphere sitting side by side with icons of Western hymnody. Britain is a bit behind.

Yet, on the fringes there are signs of a new consciousness.

In Scotland, the Wild Goose Resource Group of the Iona Community has consciously worked at making songs and prayers from the global church part of its public witness both to our incorporation in the body of Christ, and our need to express visible and audible solidarity with those elsewhere in the world whose joys and sorrows we are called to share. And it has been a particular delight to see how women of all ages and children and teenagers are immediately receptive to this material.

I think, for example, of visiting a school in the diocese of Austin, Texas where, some years previously, I had introduced musicians to songs from Africa and Asia. The diocesan director of music showed me into the gymnasium which soon filled with two hundred 5–8 year olds. It was not *Do You See This Penny?* which they sang. It was *Jesus Tawa Pano* in Shona from Zimbabwe. It was *Siyahamba* in Xhosa from South Africa. It was *Cantai ao Senhor* in Portuguese from Brazil. And all were sung with the same engagement and enthusiasm as any English language text.

But what was interesting was listening to the teachers speaking afterwards, of how they recognised a global awareness being engendered in the pupils in these formative years, as well as a true sense of the internationality of the Body of Christ.

And it will, ultimately, be the experiential rather than the abstractly theoretical which will move us and our churches from a patronising colonial mentality with regard to the universal mission of the church to the kind of reciprocal engagement of equals which John Mott first articulated on these shores almost a hundred years ago.

Yes, it will help if people realise that 'overseas or foreign songs' are a part of our heritage and revered tradition. We couldn't get through Christmas without German carols, or through Easter without French ones. When we begin Advent with *O Come O Come Immanuel*, or grace Pentecost with *Come Down O Love Divine*, we are not being autonomous Brits, we are demonstrating our reliance on continental Europe.

Inevitably the people of God move by hands-on experience. So it may be seemingly small and symbolic activities, not ostentatious ephemeral gestures, which will help us turn the corner and embrace the world. It may be the singing of a hymn from Namibia, or the placing of an Argentinian or Iraqi flag next to the Union Jack in our chancels; it may be the engagement in Bible study according to liberation theology models, or the incorporation of overseas nationals in the construction and leadership of local worship which will move us from the Black Sambos and the Reverend Richmonds of the past to full incorporation in the global church. There we will discover that God's favourite colour is not white or black but tartan.

From a lecture given in the University of Newcastle, Spring 2001

John L. Bell

...is a hymnwriter and composer based in Gasgow and working as park of the Wild Goose Resource Group of the Iona Community. With his colleagues he has produced over fifty books and recordings containing cngregational song and anthems, and dramatic, reflective and liturgical resources. He is also an occassional broadcaster on radio and television.

He lectures in liturgy and hymnody throughout Britain and abroad and in 1999 received an honorary Fellowship of the Royal School of Church Music.

Additional WGRG resources, available from
GIA Publications, Inc.:

I WILL NOT SING ALONE

Compact Disc	CD-611
Music Collection	G-6512

ONE IS THE BODY

Compact Disc	CD-513
Music Collection	G-5790

LOVE AND ANGER

Compact Disc	CD-428
Music Collection	G-4947

GOD NEVER SLEEPS

Compact Disc	CD-348
Music Collection	G-4376

THERE IS ONE AMONG US

Compact Disc	CD-460
Music Collection	G-5111

COME ALL YOU PEOPLE

Compact Disc	CD-355
Music Collection	G-4391

MANY & GREAT

Compact Disc	CD-275
Music Collection	G-3649

SENT BY THE LORD

Compact Disc	CD-276
Music Collection	G-3740

THE LAST JOURNEY
Songs for the time of grieving

Compact Disc and Reflections Book	CD-381P
Music Collection	G-4527
Compact Disc	CD-381
Reflections Book	G-4527P

The Wild Goose Resource and Worship Groups

The Wild Goose Resource Group is an expression of the Iona Community's commitment to the renewal of public worship. Based in Glasgow, the WGRG has two resource workers, John Bell and Graham Maule, who lead workshops, seminars and events throughout Britain and abroad. They are supported by Gail Ullrich (administrator) and Victoria Rudebark (sales & copyright administrator).

From 1984 to 2001, the WGRG workers were also part of the Wild Goose Worship Group. The WGWG consisted of around sixteen, predominantly lay, people at any one time, who came from a variety of occupational and denominational backgrounds. Over the 17 years of its existence, it was the WGWG who tested, as well as promoted, the material in this book.

The task of both groups has been to develop and identify new methods and materials to enable the revitalisation of congregational song, prayer and liturgy. The songs and liturgical material have now been translated and used in many countries across the world as well as being frequently broadcast on radio and television.

The WGRG, along with a committed group of fellow-Glaswegians, run HOLY CITY, a monthly ecumenical workshop and worship event for adults in the centre of Glasgow. The WGRG also publishes a mail-order catalogue, an annual Liturgy Booklet series and a twice-yearly newsletter, GOOSEgander, to enable friends and supporters to keep abreast of WGRG developments. If you would like to find out more about subscribing to these, or about ways to support the WGRG financially, please contact:

The Wild Goose Resource Group, Iona Community, Fourth Floor,
Savoy House, 140 Sauchiehall Street, Glasgow G2 3DH, Scotland.
Tel: 0141 332 6343   Fax: 0141 332 1090
e-mail: wgrg@gla.iona.org.uk   web: www.iona.org.uk/wgrg
www.wgrg.co.uk   www.holycity-glasgow.co.uk